Mali:

Malaria Operational Plan FY 2014

TABLE OF CONTENTS

EXECUTIVE SUMMARY 4

STRATEGY.. 10

INTRODUCTION 10

MALARIA SITUATION IN MALI... 11

HEALTH SYSTEM DELIVERY STRUCTURE AND MINISTRY OF HEALTH
ORGANIZATION 13

COUNTRY MALARIA CONTROL STRATEGY 16

INTEGRATION, COLLABORATION, AND COORDINATION............................ 17

PMI GOALS, TARGETS, AND INDICATORS 20

PROGRESS ON COVERAGE AND IMPACT INDICATORS TO DATE 21

CHALLENGES, OPPORTUNITIES, AND THREATS 22

PMI SUPPORT STRATEGY AND EXPECTED RESULTS................................. 23

OPERATIONAL PLAN... 24

INSECTICIDE-TREATED NETS 24

INDOOR RESIDUAL SPRAYING 28

MALARIA IN PREGNANCY... 34

CASE MANAGEMENT.. 38

Diagnostics ....*Error! Bookmark not defined.38*

Treatment 41

Pharmaceutical Management 47

BEHAVIOR CHANGE COMMUNICATIONS 50

MONITORING, EVALUATION, AND OPERATIONAL RESEARCH 52

EPIDEMIC SURVEILLANCE AND RESPONSE (ESR)..................................... 59

HEALTH SYSTEM STRENGTHENING /CAPACITY BUILDING.......................... 61

STAFFING AND ADMINISTRATION 64

TABLE 1: FY 2014 BUDGET BREAKDOWN BY PARTNER 64

TABLE 2 : FY 2014 PLANNED OBLIGATIONS 64

ACRONYMS AND ABBREVIATIONS

ACT	Artemisinin-based combination therapy
AL	Artemether-lumefantrine
ANC	Antenatal care
ASC	*Agent de Santé Communautaire* (Community Health Worker)
BCC	Behavior change communication
CDC	Centers for Disease Control and Prevention
CNIECS	National Center for Information and Communication in Health
CSCOM	*Centre de Santé Communautaire* (Community Health Center)
CSREF	*Centre de Santé de Référence* (Reference/District Health Center)
DHS	Demographic and Health Survey
DHPS	*Division d'Hygiène Publique et Salubrité* (Division of Public Hygiene and Safety)
DPM	Directorate of Drugs and Pharmacies
ESR	Epidemic surveillance and response
FANC	Focused antenatal care
Global Fund	Global Fund to Fight AIDS, Tuberculosis, and Malaria
GOM	Government of Mali
iCCM	Integrated community case management
IDP	Internally displaced person
INRSP	*Institut National de Recherche en Santé Publique* (National Institute of Public Health Research)
IPTp	Intermittent preventive treatment of pregnant women
IRS	Indoor residual spraying
ITN	Insecticide-treated bed net
IVM	Integrated vector management
LLIN	Long-lasting insecticide-treated bed net
MOH	Ministry of Health
MIP	Malaria in pregnancy
MRTC	Malaria Research and Training Center
NMCP	National Malaria Control Program
PMI	President's Malaria Initiative
PPM	*Pharmacie Populaire du Mali* (People's Pharmacy of Mali)
QA/QC	Quality assurance/quality control
RDT	Rapid diagnostic test
SLIS	*Système Local d'Information Sanitaire* (Health Management Information System)
SMC	Seasonal malaria chemoprevention
SP	Sulfadoxine-pyrimethamine
UNICEF	United Nations Children's Fund
USAID	United States Agency for International Development
USG	United States Government
WHO	World Health Organization

EXECUTIVE SUMMARY

Malaria prevention and control is a major foreign assistance objective of the U.S. Government. In May 2009, President Barack Obama announced the Global Health Initiative, a comprehensive effort to reduce the burden of disease and promote healthy communities and families around the world. Through the Global Health Initiative, the United States will help partner countries improve health outcomes, with a particular focus on improving the health of women, newborns, and children.

The President's Malaria Initiative (PMI) is a core component of the Global Health Initiative, along with family planning, maternal and child health, nutrition, HIV/AIDS, and tuberculosis. PMI was launched in June 2005 as a five-year, $1.2 billion initiative to rapidly scale up malaria prevention and treatment interventions and reduce malaria-related mortality by 50% in 15 high-burden countries in sub-Saharan Africa. With passage of the 2008 Lantos-Hyde Act, funding for PMI was extended and, as part of the GHI, the goal of PMI was adjusted to reduce malaria-related mortality by 70% in the original 15 countries by the end of 2015.

Programming of PMI activities follows the core principles of GHI: encouraging country ownership and investing in country-led plans and health systems; increasing impact and efficiency through strategic coordination and programmatic integration; strengthening and leveraging key partnerships, multilateral organizations, and private contributions; implementing a woman- and girl-centered approach; improving monitoring and evaluation; and promoting research and innovation.

PMI began supporting activities in Mali in 2007 in close collaboration with the National Malaria Control Program (NMCP) as well as international and national partners. With the *coup d'état* of March 22, 2012, in which the democratically elected president was overthrown by the military, the U.S. Government and many other donors suspended foreign aid to the Government of Mali until a democratic solution to the political crisis could be achieved. For PMI, this meant suspending all assistance and funding to the NMCP and other Ministry of Health (MOH) entities. The U.S. Department of State authorized some PMI activities on humanitarian grounds, such as procurement and distribution of essential malaria commodities; however, the bulk of PMI projects were temporarily suspended. Following intervention by the Economic Community of West African States and the international community, Malians agreed on a consensual transitional government currently in place. In late July/early August 2013, the people of Mali democratically elected a new president who was sworn in on September 4th, 2013. As a result, the U.S. Government lifted all restrictions on U.S. foreign assistance to Mali and authorized immediate return to normal bilateral relations with the Government of Mali, including direct support to the MOH.

Malaria is the primary cause of morbidity and mortality in Mali, particularly among children less than five years old. The disease is endemic to the central and southern regions (where over 90% of Mali's population lives), and considered epidemic in the north. In 2012, the national health management information system (*Système Local d'Information Sanitaire* [SLIS]), reported 2.1 million clinical cases of malaria in health facilities, accounting for 42% of all outpatient visits for all age groups. A total of 1,833 fatal malaria cases were reported, which represents 51% of all reported deaths at health facilities. However, with only 52% of suspected malaria cases at health facility confirmed by laboratory means, the SLIS data should be viewed with caution.

Since the 2006 Demographic and Health Survey (DHS), Mali has demonstrated significant progress in scaling up malaria prevention and control interventions, especially in vector control. Preliminary results from the 2012 DHS indicate a 51% reduction of under-five mortality rates from 191 deaths per 1,000 live births in 2006 DHS to 98 deaths per 1,000 live births in the 2012 DHS. Household ownership of at least one insecticide-treated bed net (ITN) increased from 50% in 2006 to 84% in 2012, and 70% of children under age five had slept under an ITN the previous night in 2012 compared with 27% in 2006. However, the same 2012 DHS survey also reported an increase in malaria parasite prevalence rates from 38% in 2010 to 52% in 2012.

Mali is the recipient of a $26 million five-year Global Fund Round 6 malaria grant to support procurement of long-lasting insecticide-treated nets (LLINs) and artemisinin-based combination therapies (ACTs) and has been approved for Phase 2 funding. However, the Round 6 grant was suspended in 2010 because of misappropriation of funds. As a result, PMI has procured emergency stocks of ACTs and rapid diagnostic tests (RDTs) to ensure sufficient quantities are available in-country. Mali's Round 10 Global Fund malaria proposal was recommended for funding; predisbursement assessment and negotiations with Population Services International, the new principal recipient, have been ongoing for the last 2.5 years and a consolidated version of the two malaria grants was signed in May 2013 with a total budget of approximately US $123 million. The consolidated grant focuses on nationwide implementation of integrated community case management and a 2015 universal LLIN campaign. During the Global Fund malaria grant negotiation process, PMI contributed to filling several commodity gaps including LLINs, ACTs, and RDTs, in order to meet the annual national needs.

While universal access to malaria prevention and control measures is the goal, pregnant women and children under five remain the focus of PMI efforts since they are the most vulnerable to malaria infection. The activities that PMI is proposing to support with FY 2014 funding align with the new 2013–2017 National Malaria Control Strategy and Plan (currently being finalized), complement activities supported in the Global Fund malaria grant, and build on investments made by PMI and other partners to improve and expand malaria-related services.

To achieve PMI's goals and targets in Mali, the following major activities will be supported with FY 2014 funding at a proposed $25 million level:

Insecticide-Treated Nets: The Malaria Strategic Plan promotes universal LLIN coverage for all age groups (defined as one LLIN for every two people). The MOH supports the provision of free LLINs distributed to target populations through two main delivery channels: mass distribution to households as part of universal coverage campaigns and routine distribution through antenatal care (ANC) and Expanded Program for Immunization clinics targeting women and infants. The NMCP has made significant progress recently toward achieving its initial goal of 80% use of LLINs among children less than five years of age and pregnant women. According to the recent 2012 DHS conducted during the peak transmission season, 84% of households owned an ITN. With funding provided in FY 2009-12, PMI procured over 3.9

million LLINs as part of a significant net contribution to a nationwide phased universal coverage campaign conducted from 2011-2013. PMI continued to support capacity building of the MOH and partners to coordinate donor inputs, track LLINs, and manage logistics and distribution systems. PMI supported the mass distribution campaign coordination activities, as well as targeted communications promoting consistent and correct LLIN use.

In FY 2014, PMI will procure 2 million nets to fill the gap for routine LLIN delivery as well as contribute to the 2015 universal coverage campaign in one region. PMI will also continue to strengthen LLIN distribution systems at the national, district, and community levels to prevent stockouts.

Indoor Residual Spraying (IRS): PMI supports the NMCP's strategy to reduce malaria transmission through targeted IRS in select high-risk areas. Since 2008, PMI has supported three IRS campaigns in the districts of Bla and Koulikoro, adding a third district (Baraoueli) in 2011. Support in 2012 included initial and refresher training of supervisors and spray operators as well as community health volunteers (*relais*); purchase of all commodities and personal protective equipment; and communication, supervision, monitoring, and environmental compliance activities. The 2012 IRS campaign was launched in mid-July, spraying approximately 203,000 houses and protecting about 700,000 residents. The 2013 IRS campaign will be launched in late summer of 2013 and will cover the same three IRS districts. With FY 2014 funding, PMI will continue to support IRS in all three districts, covering over 210,000 households. PMI will also continue strengthening the MOH's capacity to plan and supervise IRS activities within the context of its integrated vector management strategy. Other support will go to entomological monitoring related to IRS, including insecticide monitoring, insecticide resistance testing, and overall implementation of the entomological monitoring plan.

Malaria in Pregnancy: Preliminary results from the 2012 DHS showed an increased percentage of pregnant women received the recommended two doses of sulfadoxine-pyrimethamine (SP) for intermittent preventive treatment of pregnant women (IPTp) at antenatal care visits during their pregnancy (from 4% in 2006 to 20% in 2012). Coverage of IPTp2 remains low despite high antenatal care attendance rates by pregnant women: 74% visit at least once. In 2009, PMI procured 1 million sulfadoxine-pyrimethamine treatments for IPTp and in 2010 trained 1,173 health care providers in malaria in pregnancy as part of the focused antenatal care package. Communications strategies on malaria in pregnancy have targeted religious leaders, traditional leaders, grandmothers, women in positions of authority, women of childbearing age, and men. With FY 2014 funding, PMI will procure 1.8 million sulfadoxine-pyrimethamine treatments to help ensure that all pregnant women can receive at least three doses of IPTp administered as directly observed therapy. Given potential challenges in achieving IPTp targets, PMI will help expand the use of focused antenatal care training modules and increase supportive supervision of health facility staff who implement IPTp.

Case Management: Poor geographic and economic access to care is a major challenge for malaria diagnosis and treatment in Mali. Malaria diagnosis in most public-sector health facilities has been based on clinical criteria, with fewer than 10% of suspected cases of malaria having laboratory confirmation. In 2010, due to advocacy efforts of PMI and other partners, the MOH adopted significant policy changes including a community case management policy and updated severe malaria treatment and prereferral guidelines. As a result, routine health information systems data reports 52% of all suspected malaria cases were tested by microscopy or RDT in 2012, a significant improvement from 18% in 2010.

PMI continued its support of the integrated community case management of fever strategy in 2013 in five districts of Sikasso Region and expanded activities to four additional districts (two in Kayes Region and two in Segou Region). This support included training and deploying community health workers *(Agents de Santé Communautaire)*, procuring ACTs for community-based ACT distribution, and ensuring sufficient supplies of ACTs for children less than five years of age in health facilities. PMI also procured drugs for the management of severe malaria, as well as supported in-service training and supportive supervision of health workers and community health workers. The NMCP has also introduced seasonal malaria chemoprevention in selected districts targeting all children under five with four monthly rounds of a preventive treatment with sulfadoxine-pyrimethamine and amodiaquine.

With FY 2014 funding, PMI will continue to support and strengthen efforts to ensure prompt and effective case management of malaria at health facilities and support the scale-up of the integrated community case management policy nationwide. At the health facility level, PMI will concentrate on strengthening capacity in laboratory diagnostics (including quality assurance and quality control), and supply chain management. With the NMCP's scale up of seasonal malaria chemoprevention, PMI will support implementation of this new approach in one district. PMI will procure sufficient RDTs and ACTs to contribute to filling gaps in annual malaria commodity needs for health facilities and integrated community case management. PMI will strengthen quality assurance/quality control systems at national and district levels for accurate malaria diagnosis, and will support the NMCP to monitor and reinforce the correct use of ACTs at health facilities and in communities.

Behavior Change Communication (BCC): The NMCP strategy describes BCC messages targeted to vulnerable groups including pregnant women and children under five as well as families and caretakers of children, community health workers, and *relais*. The national strategy supports multiple delivery channels for messages, including mass media and interpersonal communications. PMI supports harmonization of the national BCC strategy at all levels, ensuring consistency of messages and appropriate use of all communication channels. With FY 2014 funding, PMI will support BCC activities at national and community levels to promote correct and consistent LLIN use, especially among the most vulnerable groups. PMI will continue to support engagement and mobilization of pregnant women and the promotion of malaria in pregnancy and IPTp in the community through traditional leaders and midwives. PMI will support coordination and harmonization of work among implementing partners to ensure that effective BCC messages on prompt diagnosis and early case management of malaria are promoted and disseminated.

Monitoring and Evaluation : The NMCP, with support from PMI and other partners, has developed a comprehensive national malaria monitoring and evaluation plan for 2013-2017, including capacity building, improvement of data collection, and provision of equipment to collect and analyze data. The quality of routine data collection, analysis and reporting through the health information system is variable and feedback is not delivered in a timely manner for program management. At present, population-based surveys provide the most accurate data on malaria in Mali, and have recently shown tremendous progress especially for ITN ownership and use. In 2012, PMI supported a DHS that included anemia and parasitemia estimates on a national level. Preliminary results indicate that while anemia has remained relatively constant for children 6-59 months at 82% (hemoglobin<11g/dL), parasitemia in the same age group has increased from 38% in 2010 to 52% in 2012.

With FY 2014 funding, PMI will support preparations for a national Malaria Indicator Survey in 2015 to provide follow-up data on key malaria indicators along with anemia and parasitemia. Efforts will continue to strengthen the SLIS through training and supervision, with a focus on the community health center level (*Centres de Santé Communautaire*). Activities will also focus on the integration of integrated community case management data into the SLIS. PMI is supporting two operations research activities: a project to evaluate the impact of LLINs treated with dual insecticides to inform PMI about the potential ability of this new LLIN variety to affect malaria transmission in areas with high pyrethroid resistance; and an evaluation of the seasonal malaria chemoprevention intervention to determine its relative usefulness as part of the malaria control strategy in Mali.

Epidemic Surveillance and Response: Mali's epidemic surveillance and response system features weekly disease-reporting procedures from 13 districts in the epidemic-prone northern region. While gradually improving in recent years, data analysis capacity is still weak and epidemic response plans will need reinforcement especially following the events of March 2012. To ensure accurate malaria case reporting, laboratory confirmation is also required as many malaria cases are treated presumptively. In 2008 and 2009, PMI procured ACTs and IRS supplies to be stored in two of the regions as contingency in the event of an epidemic. These supplies were rotated back into the supply chain management system for use before expiration. The current practice is to respond to epidemics with available existing stocks and supplies stored at national level. With FY 2013 and FY 2014 funding, PMI will strengthen epidemic surveillance and response capacity in epidemic-prone areas through a collaborative process with the NMCP and the World Health Organization to reach consensus on appropriate epidemic thresholds; strengthen current data sources for malaria epidemic detection; develop revised reporting mechanisms; train local health officers to analyze and monitor malaria data; and ensure appropriate epidemic response procedures are in place. Assistance will also focus on training to health care providers for diagnostics, case reporting, data analysis and monitoring, and case management. Periodic supervisory visits will verify that health workers use RDTs and microscopy adequately, report in a timely fashion, and perform case management appropriately. Implementation of epidemic surveillance and response activities in the north is contingent upon political stability and accessibility in this region.

Health System Strengthening / Capacity Building: Since its first year, PMI has contributed substantially to building capacity of the NMCP and other Government of Mali entities through direct funding of specific activities. This support has allowed the government's partners to improve training, supervision and quality assurance and quality control for diagnostics; to oversee implementation of BCC activities related to malaria; and to improve partner coordination. With the *coup* in 2012, PMI suspended direct funding for NMCP capacity-building efforts and focused on strengthening the health system at the community level. Pending the resumption of U.S. Government activities in FY 2014, PMI intends to resume direct funding support to the NMCP to reach coverage targets for key malaria interventions. Collaboration will continue with other partners to support NMCP structure and staff, specifically to increase capacity at all levels to plan, implement, supervise, forecast commodity needs; improve distribution systems; coordinate with partners; and monitor and evaluate malaria prevention and control activities. In addition, PMI will continue training and mentoring NMCP staff to increase their skills in data analysis, interpretation, and reporting of findings both from routine supervision and from other data sources such as large household and health facility surveys.

STRATEGY

INTRODUCTION

The President's Malaria Initiative (PMI) is a core component of the Global Health Initiative (GHI), along with HIV/AIDS, and tuberculosis. PMI was launched in June 2005 as a 5-year, $1.2 billion initiative to rapidly scale up malaria prevention and treatment interventions and reduce malaria-related mortality by 50% in 15 high-burden countries in sub-Saharan Africa. With passage of the 2008 Lantos-Hyde Act, funding for PMI was extended and, as part of the GHI, the goal of PMI was adjusted to reduce malaria-related mortality by 70% in the original 15 countries by the end of 2015. This will be achieved by continuing to scale up coverage of the most vulnerable groups — children under five years of age and pregnant women — with proven preventive and therapeutic interventions, including artemisinin-based combination therapies (ACTs), insecticide-treated nets (ITNs), intermittent preventive treatment of pregnant women (IPTp), and indoor residual spraying (IRS).

Mali was selected as a PMI country in FY 2007. This FY 2014 Malaria Operational Plan presents a detailed implementation plan for Mali, based on the PMI Multi-Year Strategy and Plan and the National Malaria Control Program's 5-Year Strategy.

In 2015, the population of Mali will reach approximately 17.9 million, with more than 47% less than 15 years of age; children under the age of five represent 17% of the total population.[1] Approximately 64% of Malians live in poverty (i.e., on less than US$1 a day). In 2010, the estimated annual gross national income per capita was just $600 (World Bank, 2010), making Mali one of the world's poorest countries.

Since March 2012, Mali has been in political turmoil after the democratically elected president was overthrown in a military *coup d'état*, plunging the government into a constitutional crisis. At the same time, various rebel groups in northern Mali took advantage of the political instability to occupy the three northern regions (which represent one-third of the country). The ensuing violence caused some 400,000 people to be displaced either as refugees to neighboring countries or as internally displaced persons (IDPs) in the southern regions. In response to the *coup*, the U.S. Government (USG) and many other donors suspended foreign aid to the Government of Mali (GOM) until a democratic solution to the political crisis could be achieved. For the President's Malaria Initiative (PMI), this meant suspending all assistance and funding to the National Malaria Control Program (NMCP) and other Ministry of Health (MOH) entities, except for some PMI activities, such as procurement and distribution of essential malaria commodities, which were authorized by the U.S. Department of State on humanitarian grounds. Following the intervention of the Economic Community of West African States and the international community, Mali agreed on a transitional government. In late July/early August 2013, the people of Mali democratically elected a new president who was sworn in on September 4th, 2013. As a result, the USG lifted all restrictions on U.S. foreign assistance to Mali and authorized a immediate return to normal bilateral relations with the GOM including direct support to the MOH.

---

1 Extrapolated from the 2011 General Census, using a 3% growth per year projection

This document briefly reviews the current status of malaria control policies and interventions in Mali, describes progress to date, identifies challenges and unmet needs if the targets of the NMCP and PMI are to be achieved, and provides a description of planned FY 2014 activities.

MALARIA SITUATION IN MALI

Malaria is the primary cause of morbidity and mortality in Mali, particularly for children less than five years old. In 2012, the national health information system (*Système Local d'Information Sanitaire* or [SLIS]) reported 2.1 million clinical cases of malaria in health facilities, accounting for 42% of all outpatient visits for all age groups. A total of 1,833 fatal malaria cases were reported. However, with only 52% of suspected malaria cases at facility level confirmed by test, SLIS data should be viewed with caution. According to the 2012 Demographic and Health Survey (DHS), the prevalence of malaria among children under five years of age was 52% based on microscopy and 47% based on rapid diagnostic tests (RDTs) (results based on 12,000 households and 6,500 children under five years of age surveyed).

Plasmodium falciparum accounts for 85-90% of malaria infections, while *P. malariae* (10-14%) and *P. ovale* (1%) make up the remainder. A 2004 study conducted by the Malaria Research and Training Center (MRTC) in Menaka, an epidemic-prone region in the north, indicated a prevalence of *P. vivax* of 8%, which was confirmed by polymerase chain reaction.

Malaria is endemic to the central and southern regions, where about 90% of Mali's population lives, and it is epidemic in the north due to the limited viability of *Anopheles* species in the desert climate. Malaria transmission varies in Mali's five geoclimatic zones. It occurs year-round in the Sudano-Guinean zone in the south, with a seasonal peak between June and November. The transmission season is shorter in the northern Sahelian zone, lasting approximately three to four months (July/August to October). Malaria transmission is endemic in the Niger River Delta and areas around dams with rice cultivation, and is endemic with low transmission in urban areas including Bamako and Mopti. Epidemics occur in the north (Tombouctou, Gao, and Kidal Regions) and in the northern districts of Kayes, Koulikoro, Segou and Mopti Regions; the last epidemic was identified in November 2012 in Tombouctou.

In 2012 the country registered a record-setting rainfall; this may partially explain the high prevalence of parasitemia observed during the 2012 DHS. The figure below shows Mali's average rainfall density from 2007 to 2012.

Figure 1. Average rainfall density, Mali, 2007 to 2012

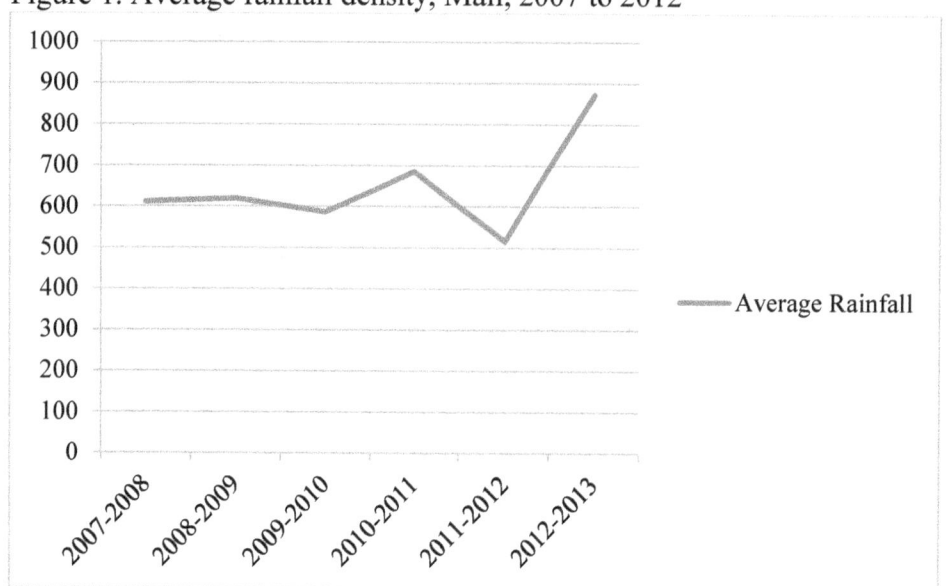

Note: Rainfall ranges from 62mm in Aguelhoc in 2011 (Kidal Region) to 1377mm in Kolondiebain (Sikasso Region) in 2012.

With the recent insecurity in the north, almost 300,000 IDPs have migrated from the north to the south and are at risk of severe disease and death from malaria because of their low immunity to malaria infections. Parasite prevalence in the Mopti Region, which borders the northern regions and has received the majority of the IDPs, has increased from 47% to 71%.

HEALTH SYSTEM DELIVERY STRUCTURE AND MINISTRY OF HEALTH ORGANIZATION

At the national level, Mali's MOH is composed of the cabinet of the minister of health and national directorates reporting directly to the secretary general of the MOH. The NMCP was established in 1993 under the oversight of the Disease Control Division of the National Health Directorate . In July 2007, the GOM elevated the NMCP to a directorate level in the MOH organizational structure. The NMCP director supervises four technical divisions and one administrative and finance division, and reports directly to the secretary general of the MOH. Due to its new higher profile in the MOH, the NMCP can now participate in and influence decision-making about malaria control more effectively, including development of MOH work plans and budgets.

Mali is divided into eight administrative regions (Kayes, Koulikoro, Sikasso, Ségou, Mopti, Gao, Tombouctou, and Kidal) plus the capital, Bamako. Each represents a regional health directorate. The regions are subdivided into 49 administrative *"cercles"* comprised of 54 health districts, and Bamako is divided into six administrative communes that correspond to six health districts; thus the country has a total of 60 health districts. Governance is decentralized into 703 communes, each one administered by an elected local council headed by a mayor. The organization of the health system is based upon the principles of decentralization of health services and community participation to extend health service coverage and to ensure access to essential and effective medicines.

The health delivery system is composed of three levels:
- The central level with five national reference hospitals The intermediate level with eight regional hospitals (Kayes, Kati, Sikasso, Ségou, Mopti, Tombouctou, Gao, and the maternal and child hospital of Bamako)
- The local level with 60 referral health centers (*Centre de Santé de Référence* [CSREF]) constituting the district reference level

A total of 1,134 functional community health centers (*Centre de Santé Communautaire* [CSCOM]) as well as parastatal, faith-based, military, and other private health centers, make up the community health services level. The CSCOMs are established and managed by community health associations.

The MOH has a critical staff shortage at all levels of the public health system, especially for service provision below the national level. In addition, health workers are not distributed proportionally to population throughout the country. In 2012, the national ratio of doctors to the population was 1:8,528, with rural regions having less than one doctor for every 24,000 inhabitants. Regional directors oversee health teams that implement integrated health interventions; currently all regional teams have malaria focal persons. The CSREF (at the district level) is the first referral structure for CSCOMs; the district health team is headed by a medical chief responsible for technical supervision of CSCOMs and has a malaria focal person as well. The community health associations manage CSCOM staff and operations; collect proceeds from drug sales, consultations, and user fees; and pay salaries and other expenses. As is the case at the central level, distribution of staff is uneven. In 2009, the percentage of CSCOMs headed by a certified head nurse was close to the World Health Organization (WHO) norms and ranged from 100% in five regions to 95% in Kayes. The number of staff employed depends on the level of community resources to pay them. In 2011, The MOH started the "medicalization" of CSCOMs, meaning the appointment of qualified medical doctors in CSCOMs. According to the strategic plan for health and social development (2013-2022), in 2011, 30% of CSCOMs were headed by a medical doctor.

In 2010, Mali approved an integrated community case management (iCCM) package offered by community health workers (*Agents de Santé Communautaires* [ASCs]) to provide health services at the community level. The ASCs, who receive a financial incentive or salaries from the local government and different partners for their services, provide free treatment for uncomplicated malaria, acute respiratory infections, diarrhea, and micronutrient supplementation. The ASCs also provide primary care to newborns and family planning for eligible families. Based on national iCCM directives, the iCCM package and ASC model will be introduced in villages located 5 km or more from a health facility and will cover 2-3 villages in a radius of 3 km with a catchment area of approximately 1,500 people. This iCCM approach and ASC efforts will be supported by an additional cadre of community health volunteers, the *relais*, whose role is to carry out behavior change communication activities (BCC) and health education to promote key health messages to complement iCCM activities. Support for the GOM scale-up plan for nationwide implementation of the iCCM package including supervision, commodity management, RDT confirmation, and quality assurance/quality control (QA/QC) were incorporated into Round 10 grant of the Global Fund to Fight AIDS, Tuberculosis, and Malaria (Global Fund). As of May 2013, a total of 1,847 ASCs had been trained and are fully functional; an estimated 4,758 community health workers are needed to achieve full coverage of iCCM activities.

Health Financing Through Cost Recovery

Mali has a strong cost recovery system that is based on the Bamako Initiative. At the district level, communities can establish CSCOMs based on the following criteria: the establishment of a community health association; raising a minimum of 10% of the cost of construction or renovation of the health facility; and the hiring and support of health personnel. All CSCOMs are required to deliver the national minimum package of services comprising of curative, preventive and promotional health activities. Once authorized by the district medical officer, the MOH provides an initial stock of medicines, consumables, and equipment. In principle, communes are expected to allocate 15% of their budget for social services including water, education, and health.

CSCOMs have three forms of revenue generation that are managed by the community health association: membership fees, sales of essential drugs, and fees for services. Service fees vary by health area and are set by the community health association after consultation with the population. Membership fees allow for reduced service charges at some CSCOMs. Funds derived from the sale of medications are kept in a separate account to prevent providers from overprescribing to generate revenue and to prevent decapitalization of pharmacy stock. The community health association management committee purchases replacement drugs for the CSCOM through the national pharmacy system or from approved private sector companies based on availability. Selected drugs (e.g., antimalarials for children under five and pregnant women, vitamin A, and immunization services) are provided free by the government or donors. The CSCOMs must finance the transportation of their drugs from CSREFs. However, due to small profit margins and the loss of or use of revenues for non-pharmaceutical purposes, CSCOM drug stores often lack available funds to cover these costs.

National Financial Planning for Malaria and Health/Social Development

The NMCP receives annual budget support from the National Health and Social Development Program. Its Evaluation Committee manages and approves the annual operating budget plan. Several partners (including the governments of the Netherlands, Sweden, and Canada) provide direct budget support on an annual basis. Other donors, including the USG, target their funding to sub-sectors and specific programs. The GOM contributes mostly to salaries, office space, and other operating costs in the program's annual budget, but also procures malaria commodities such as artemisinin-based combination therapy (ACTs), RDTs, severe malaria drugs, and long-lasting insecticide-treated bed nets (LLINs). The GOM, local governments, community health associations and other donor partners, such as the Global Alliance for Vaccines and Immunizations (GAVI) are supporting the salaries of CSCOM's staff, including qualified medical doctors. While GOM increased its annual investment in malaria control from about $1 million in FY 2007, $6.7 million in FY 2008, and $9 million in FY 2009, this support decreased to approximately $4 million in FY 2010, $3 million in FY 2011, and $2.5 million in 2012.

COUNTRY MALARIA CONTROL STRATEGY

The NMCP establishes strategies for all malaria interventions; coordinates research; proposes policies, norms, and guidelines; and coordinates partner work plans. The NMCP also supports decentralized regional and district health teams through training and supervision. The 2007-2011 NMCP Strategic Plan was reviewed in early 2012 and a new five-year plan (2013-2017) was developed by the NMCP and partners in 2013. Its goal is to "reduce the burden of malaria to a level that will not constitute a major cause of morbidity and mortality nor a barrier to economic and social development."

The new NMCP Strategic Plan aims to achieve the following targets by 2015:
- Reduce malaria mortality to near zero
- Reduce malaria morbidity by at least 75% as compared to 2000 levels
- Reinforce/strengthen the NMCP coordination and management capacity

Expected results to be achieved by the 2013-2017 strategic plan are as follows:
- At least 80% of the population at risk of malaria is using LLINs including pregnant women and children under five years old;
- At least 80% of pregnant women have received three sulfadoxine-pyrimethamine (SP) doses as intermittent preventive treatment of pregnant women (IPTp) during their pregnancy;
- At least 80% of children under five received the four full courses of seasonal malaria chemoprevention (SMC) in selected zones;
- At least 90% of suspected malaria cases are confirmed using microscopy or RDTs before treatment, at all levels of the health system including the CHW level;
- At least 90% of confirmed malaria cases receive appropriate malaria treatment both for severe and uncomplicated cases as indicated in the national guidelines;
- At least 80% of the population is protected by indoor residual spraying (IRS) in IRS target zones;
- At least 80% of the general population knows what tools are on recommended to prevent malaria. ; At least 90% of emergency cases and malaria epidemics are detected in the following two weeks and receive an appropriate response.

Due to the diversity of malaria transmission in Mali (largely endemic in the south and epidemic-prone in the north), the strategic plan emphasizes nationwide universal coverage of key malaria interventions for prevention and control of malaria, as well as specific interventions such as epidemic and entomological surveillance and targeted operational research in areas with unstable malaria transmission. The main interventions in the new national strategic plan for 2013-2017 include:

- Ensure universal access to malaria prevention tools for 100% of the population at risk including use of LLINs, IPTp for pregnant women, and SMC for children under five.
- Ensure protection of 100% of the population with IRS in targeted areas;
- Ensure 100% diagnostic confirmation using microscopy or RDTs at all levels including the CHW level;

- Ensure correct case management of 100% of malaria confirmed cases at all levels including the community level;
- Strengthen the sentinel surveillance systems (epidemiological and entomological) in areas with unstable malaria transmission;
- Strengthen the integrated disease surveillance system in all districts and hospitals to collect weekly malaria data for prompt decision making;
- Strengthen BCC in order to increase the use of prevention tools and promote early care seeking for patients with fever;
- Revitalize the monitoring and evaluation and surveillance interventions by introducing a functional routine surveillance system at all the levels of the health system;
- Strengthen the operational research through studies and surveys on malaria;
- Revitalize and strengthen the national Roll Back Malaria partnership to leverage sustainable funds for malaria activities;
- Reinforce regional malaria coordination and collaboration;
- Reinforce managerial capacity of the NMCP and coordination mechanisms at all levels of the health pyramid.

The NMCP updated its national policy to reflect two new WHO recommendations: implementation of SMC in the Sahel zones and administration of monthly IPTp-SP to pregnant women at every ANC visit after the first trimester. In 2012, the NMCP with support from the nongovernmental organization *Médecins Sans Frontières* (MSF) piloted SMC in one district, administering a monthly treatment of SP and AQ to children under five during the peak malaria transmission period (August – October). The NMCP is expanding SMC to six additional districts in 2013 with support from the United Nations Children's Fund (UNICEF) for commodities. Based on results of the pilot, PMI plans to support implementation and evaluation of SMC in one district.

INTEGRATION, COLLABORATION, AND COORDINATION

Communications among malaria control partners in Mali are coordinated through the NMCP monthly partners' meetings. Malaria control is part of the national sector-wide approach, based on a strategic Ten-Year Plan for Social and Health Development and operationalized through the five-year National Health and Social Development Program. The plan is supported by the Financial and Technical Partners' Forum, which meets monthly to share information on ongoing programs, new initiatives, strategies, and policies; to coordinate interventions; and to help leverage resources. The NMCP is responsible for overseeing all malaria control activities conducted in Mali, but cites partner and donor coordination as one of its biggest challenges. The NMCP seeks better mechanisms for ensuring increased partner information sharing around key activities.

Funding

Key funding and technical partners to the NCMP include the Global Fund, WHO, UNICEF, the World Bank, and the USG. The U.S. National Institutes of Health also supports the MRTC within the Faculty of Medicine at the University of Bamako. At the implementation level, partners include numerous nongovernmental and private voluntary organizations including

Groupe Pivot Santé, the National Federation of Community Health Associations (*Fédération Nationale des Associations de Santé Communautaire*), Doctors without Borders (*Médecins Sans Frontières*), World Vision, and Plan International. Partner funding activities include the following:

- UNICEF implements iCCM (including malaria diagnosis and case management) in 30 health districts and provides LLINs, ACTs, and RDTs to the three northern regions (Tombouctou, Gao, and Kidal);
- World Vision provided 470,000 LLINs to implement the universal coverage LLIN campaign in two districts in Koulikoro and Kayes Regions;
- The Muskoka Initiative, funded by the Canadian International Development Agency (CIDA), is implementing iCCM in four districts in the Sikasso Region that are not already covered by PMI;
- CIDA is procuring ACTs for the implementation of iCCM in the Segou Region;
- WHO provides technical assistance in malaria with the development of Global Fund proposals and the development of new NMCP and MOH policy and strategy documents.

Mali's Global Fund Round 6 Phase 2 grant for malaria and its Global Fund tuberculosis grant were suspended in 2010 based on the Global Fund Inspector General's (IG) identification of misuse of approximately US $5.3 million from the tuberculosis and malaria grants. The GOM has been responsive to Global Fund IG concerns and has taken steps to rectify the situation by replacing the Minister of Health and making a commitment to provide a reimbursement plan and timeline. Unfortunately, the destruction of MOH offices during the recent *coup d'état* has delayed the submission of these documents. Due to the misuse of funds, Global Fund and the MOH selected a new principal recipient, Population Services International, to manage the Global Fund grants. The approved Round 10 malaria grant and the Round 6 Phase 2 grant have been consolidated into one malaria grant, which was signed in May 2013. The consolidated malaria grant supports scaling up iCCM implementation, procurement of ACTs and RDTs, and support for a universal LLIN coverage campaign in 2015. The total budget amount under this grant is approximately $121 million with $60 million available in the first three years.

GHI and Other USG Programs

Malaria prevention and control is a major foreign assistance objective of the USG. In 2009, President Obama announced the Global Health Initiative (GHI), a six-year, comprehensive effort to reduce the burden of disease and promote healthy communities and families around the world. The GHI is a global commitment to invest in healthy and productive lives, building upon and expanding the USG's successes in addressing specific diseases and issues. The President's Malaria Initiative (PMI) is a core component of the GHI, along with HIV/AIDs and Tuberculosis (TB).

The U.S. Agency for International Development (USAID)/Mali has provided direct funding to the MOH, including PMI funding to support the NMCP and its priority activities. However, no USG funding was provided during FY 2012 and FY 2013 due to restrictions following the *coup d'état*. USAID/Mali supported a team of two accountants and an auditor at the MOH to oversee all USG funding and ensure that all USG requirements are applied. USG funds are disbursed in small increments following a review of the MOH work plans and justifications. These funds are audited annually and the results shared with USAID's Regional Office of the Inspector General in Dakar. The audits have revealed no misuse of USG funds. USG support to GOM is expected to resume when there are democratic elections and an established democratic government.

As a USG Feed the Future country (2011-2016), Mali is implementing a coordinated government strategy to address food security and nutrition issues. Anemia, due to iron deficiency, malaria, and helminth infections, affects over 80% of children under five nationwide and exceeds 90% in some regions (e.g., Sikasso). The GOM is committed to developing multisectorial programs that address access to health care to improve overall dietary intake and disease status of Malians. PMI will discuss opportunities for collaboration with Feed the Future and GHI to improve maternal and child health services and coordinate on relevant malaria and nutrition BCC messages.

Private Sector Partnerships

The NMCP and PMI maintain working relationships with several members of the private sector:
- The NMCP has recently partnered with the Association of Employers and Business Owners (*Patronnat du Mali*) including the bank sector. During the World Malaria Day 2013 celebration, the members of the *Patronnat* held malaria prevention awareness events and pledged to provide free nets to their employees and their dependents. During the World Malaria Day celebration, the International Bank of Mali provided free nets to its employees and family members.
- The NMCP has a long-established collaboration with bed-net vendors in the country. With the country's well-established net culture, net vendors in Mali enjoy a large market in both urban and rural areas. During the malaria day celebration, a private net vendor company distributed free nets to pregnant women and newborns in one commune in Bamako.
- Private clinics, pharmacies, and laboratories are becoming more prevalent with a larger presence in urban areas. To date, the NMCP has provided them with diagnosis and malaria case management information based on country guidelines. The NMCP plans to train and supervise their personnel in order to ensure they understand and apply the national directives related to malaria diagnostics and treatment. PMI and the USAID/Mali mission will support efforts to strengthen medical practices, including the testing and treatment of malaria, of private pharmacies.
- The mining industry is growing in Mali. Currently, at least five mining companies are supporting IRS activities in their employees' residence sites and neighboring villages. PMI will continue to facilitate a dialogue between the NMCP and the mining companies to ensure that they adhere to national and international IRS standards and to promote best practices, such as entomological surveillance. PMI and the NMCP are in discussions with Rand Gold Resources, a mining company, to fund the implementation of SMC in one entire district and to cover the surrounding villages at another mining site in 2013.

PMI GOALS, TARGETS, AND INDICATORS

The goal of PMI is to reduce malaria-associated mortality by 70% compared to pre-initiative levels in the 15 original PMI countries. By the end of 2015, PMI will assist Mali to achieve the following targets in populations at risk for malaria:

- >90% of households with a pregnant woman and/or children under five will own at least one insecticide-treated net (ITN)
- 85% of children under five will have slept under an ITN the previous night
- 85% of pregnant women will have slept under an ITN the previous night
- 85% of houses in geographic areas targeted for IRS will have been sprayed
- 85% of pregnant women and children under five will have slept under an ITN the previous night or in a house that has been protected by IRS
- 85% of women who have completed a pregnancy in the last two years will have received two or more doses of IPTp during that pregnancy

PROGRESS ON COVERAGE AND IMPACT INDICATORS TO DATE

Mali has made significant progress on malaria control in the past decade and has seen subsequent gains in child survival. The under-five mortality decreased from 191 deaths per 1,000 live births in the 2006 DHS to 98 deaths per 1,000 live births in the 2012 DHS, representing a reduction in under-five deaths of 51%. However, there is still much work to be done in order to reach the intervention coverage targets established by NMCP and PMI.

Indicator	DHS 2006	Anemia and parasitemia survey 2010	Other data sources	DHS 2012*
Proportion of households with at least one ITN	50%	85%	-	84%
Proportion of children less than five years old who slept under an ITN the previous night	27%	70%	-	70%
Proportion of pregnant women who slept under an ITN the previous night	29%	-	55% (2010 Multiple Indicator Cluster Survey)	75%
Proportion of households in targeted zones reached by IRS	-	-	97% (2011 RTI coverage data)	98% (2012 Abt coverage data)

Proportion of women who received two or more doses of IPTp during their last pregnancy in the last 2 years	4%	-	32% (HMIS 2012)	20%
Proportion of children less than five years old with fever in the last two weeks who received treatment with ACT within 24 hours of onset of fever	-	8%	-	9%
Any anemia (<11g/dL) Severe anemia (<8g/dL)	81% 10%	85% 26%	-	82% 9%
Parasite prevalence (microscopy/RDT)	-	38%/43%	-	52%/47%**

* Preliminary results subject to change as of June 2013; sampling excluded the three northern districts.
** National estimate that excludes the lower-prevalence northern region.

RELEVANT EVIDENCE OF PROGRESS

Following its adoption of universal coverage goals, Mali launched a rolling phased campaign in April 2011 to achieve 100% ownership and 80% use of LLINs in the general population, and to replace old nets distributed in 2006. An estimated 8.67 million nets were originally required based on a population of 15.6 million people. As of June 2013, PMI has procured and distributed a total of 6.1million LLINs and by October 2013 an additional 3.070 million LLINs procured by PMI will be available for a mass campaign in Kayes and for nationwide routine distribution at health facilities. A mass campaign targeting LLINs for the population living in Bamako will be covered by the Global Fund.

Over the past year, RDTs were scaled up nationwide, leading to increased levels of confirmed testing. The 2012 SLIS reported 52% of all suspected malaria cases have been tested by microscopy or RDT, compared with 32% in 2011 and 18% in 2010. The 2012 health facility survey found that about half of suspect malaria cases were diagnostically confirmed: 63% of children under five years with suspected malaria were tested with either microscopy or RDT, while 47% of over-five patients with suspected malaria were tested at these facilities. In addition, according to a new short message service (SMS)-based reporting system piloted in two districts, the percentage of suspected fever cases tested by microscopy or RDT between October 2012 and March 2013 has reached 88%.

Since PMI's launch in 2007 in Mali, impressive gains in child survival have been noticed; all-cause under-five-mortality fell from 191 deaths per 1000 live births in 2006 DHS to 98 deaths per 1000 live births in the 2012 DHS. This represents a reduction of under-five deaths by 51%. Since malaria is the number one cause of mortality among children under five, these results are likely due to the success of malaria control efforts. The preliminary results from the 2012 DHS show mixed evidence of progress for the malaria control program. Coverage of key interventions has remained steady since 2010 and in some cases increased despite the political turmoil of 2012/2013. Household ownership of ITN remained constant at 84%, one of the highest coverage levels among PMI countries and a major achievement given the instability in the country. ITN use among children under-five also remained steady at 70%, while use among pregnant women increased from 55% in 2010 to 75% in 2012. There was likewise an increase in the percentage of women receiving two doses of IPTp from 4% in 2006 to 20% in 2012. In terms of impact, the percentage of children with severe anemia (<8g/dl) fell from 26% in 2010 to 9% in 2012. However, the same survey's preliminary figures on parasitemia indicate an increase in prevalence from 38% in 2010 to 52% in 2012. There are many hypotheses as to why the high levels of coverage have not translated to reductions in parasitemia in this age group. Mali experienced record-setting rainfall in 2012 just prior to the field work for the survey which may have acted as a catalyst to transmission. In addition, the sampling frame for the anemia and parasitemia survey included the low transmission regions of the North in the denominator, whereas the DHS 2012 excluded the North because of the instability. Thus, the higher level of parasitemia in 2012 might be partially derived from a difference in sampling frames between the two surveys. Finally, the high transmission zones of southern Mali have seen an influx of IDPs from the low malaria burden areas of the North. These IDPs do not have acquired immunity to malaria and may exhibit higher parasite prevalence. PMI is supporting secondary analysis efforts to explore these hypotheses and provide some explanation for the higher levels of anemia and parasitemia in the face of a successful control effort.

CHALLENGES, OPPORTUNITIES, AND THREATS

Recent political and security instability, persistent issues related to NMCP capacity, and challenges in coordinating donor funding conspire to threaten Malians' access to malaria prevention and treatment interventions. The situation in Mali is dynamic, however, and with a thorough understanding of these challenges, PMI can leverage resources, both technical and financial, to address these threats.

Two specific issues posed major challenges to malaria activities in general, and PMI activities specifically:

- Security issues particularly in the three northern regions of Gao, Tombouctou, and Kidal, which were recently freed by the French and MISMA (Mission to support Mali). This situation limited the ability of the NMCP to implement and monitor malaria activities in those regions where the population has low immunity to malaria and limited access to quality malaria services. In addition, data collection activities for the 2012 DHS were not able to take place in the three northern regions and the routine data collection for HMIS was discontinued during the long period of occupation by rebel groups. The security situation improved considerably after the rebels were driven out by international forces and with the progressive installation of Malian authorities in the northern regions. The country anticipates that as the region stabilizes, proposed activities, such as epidemic surveillance and response (ESR), can be resumed.

- Mali's southern regions comprise the hyperendemic malaria zone and have received more than 300,000 IDPs from the northern regions. This presents a logistical problem in many ways: the need to plan and budget commodities for an increased IDP population in Mopti and other southern cities and the real possibility of epidemics of malaria due to the lower immunity of the IDPs who have not been exposed to endemic malaria previously. PMI's FY 2012 and FY 2013 funding is being reprogrammed to address some of these concerns.

The NMCP has several administrative and managerial issues to resolve, including:

- Inadequate office space and inefficient electricity supply and internet connectivity;
- Insufficient qualified staff at all levels;
- Inefficient supply chain management systems where malaria drugs are often available at national and regional levels but not at the health facilities and community level;
- Difficulty coordinating multiple donor partners with different agendas;
- Limited access to primary health care in Mali;
- Despite some progress in routine system strengthening, the quality and use of HMIS data still has major issues including timeliness, completeness, and accuracy, and data are not routinely used to inform decision-making.

The Mali team has taken these challenges into consideration during the FY 2014 MOP planning process. Proposed activities seek to address these issues, including continued M&E support for routine system strengthening, supply chain management, and continued implementation of iCCM to increase community access to health care.

Finally, the 2.5 year suspension of the Global Fund malaria grant activities and disbursement of funding created additional challenges in ensuring that adequate malaria prevention and control measures are in place for the population. Mali's Global Fund consolidated malaria grant (Round 6 Phase 2 and Round 10) is now signed with a new principal recipient (Population Services International) which will increase malaria prevention and control efforts in Mali and procurements of key malaria commodities, including LLINs, ACTs, RDTs, and laboratory microscopy kits. PMI will work closely with the Global Fund and the new Principal Recipient to coordinate these efforts.

PMI SUPPORT STRATEGY AND EXPECTED RESULTS

PMI will support the NMCP and its key objective in malaria control by filling gaps in commodity procurement to ensure the availability of LLINs, RDTs, ACTs, and SP at the local level and bolstering the supply chain to avoid future stockouts. PMI funds will be used to update and develop skills in diagnostics and case management among providers, principally at the community and CSCOM levels, but also throughout the health system. The overall health system will be strengthened through improved approaches to monitoring and evaluation, including enhancements to the routine HMIS and training of health care providers and managers on use of data for decision-making. Operational research activities will be undertaken to fine-tune program implementation for the Malian context. Finally, all the service provision improvements will be supported through a strong program of BCC to improve knowledge about malaria control in the communities.

Some of the expected results of the PMI program include:

Prevention:
1. PMI will support targeted IRS spraying in three districts, protecting a population of approximately 760,000 people.
2. PMI will procure approximately 2 million LLINs: 1.4 million LLINs to launch the 2015 mass campaign in Segou to maintain universal coverage, and 600,000 LLINs to be

distributed during ANC and Expanded Program on Immunization clinics to cover gaps in target populations through the routine system nationwide.

3. PMI will procure 1.8 million SP treatments to contribute to the annual needs for the proportion of the approximately 900,000 pregnant women in Mali who attend ANC.

Case management:

1. PMI will procure approximately 1.2 million artemether-lumefantrine (AL) treatments, 1.5 million RDTs, and 300,000 treatment packs of injectable artesunate, which will be used for treatment of severe malaria. These commodities will ensure prompt and effective treatment of malaria cases at facility and community levels as well as contribute to epidemic preparedness and response. These figures are based on the assumption that Global Fund and GOM are procuring additional stocks to meet the country's annual commodity needs.

2. PMI will support implementation of iCCM in the three regions: Kayes, Sikasso, and Koulikoro. The other regions will be covered by Global Fund, UNICEF, and CIDA. The scale-up coverage of iCCM will contribute to increased access to health care for children under five.

3. PMI will implement SMC in three districts in Kayes Region, reaching approximately 150,000 children under five with four monthly treatments of SP and amodiaquine.

OPERATIONAL PLAN

INSECTICIDE-TREATED NETS

NMCP/PMI Objectives

The MOH supports the provision of free LLINs distributed to target populations through two main delivery channels: mass distribution to households as part of universal coverage campaigns and routine distribution through antenatal care (ANC) and child immunization clinics. Mali defines achievement of universal coverage as one LLIN for every two persons. Since 2006, the MOH has provided free LLINs to children less than five years of age in an integrated campaign and through a phased national universal coverage campaign for all susceptible populations. To sustain coverage, the MOH seeks to provide free nets to pregnant women at their first ANC visit and to infants when they complete their national immunization series.

Progress during the last 12 months

Traditionally Mali has had a strong culture of net ownership and use; ownership of at least one net per household is high and the use of nets in the vulnerable population is even higher. According to the 2012 DHS survey conducted during the peak transmission season, 84% of households owned at least one LLIN and 70% of children under five and 75% pregnant women slept under a LLIN the previous night. These findings suggest that Mali has not only its maintained high net ownership since December 2007, but has increased coverage.

Following its adoption of universal coverage goals, Mali launched a rolling, phased campaign in April 2011 to achieve 100% ownership and 80% use of LLINs in the general population, and to replace old nets distributed in 2006. The NMCP and partners opted for a phased approach to the campaign, starting with Sikasso Region and proceeding to other regions until sufficient resources were available to cover the entire country. An estimated 8.67 million nets were originally required based on a population of 15.6 million. As of June 2013, more than 4.4 million LLINs had been distributed in five of nine regions, of which PMI provided more than 3.9 million LLINs for distribution in Sikasso, Segou and Mopti regions. UNICEF will provide 70,000 nets for the three northern regions. PMI will complete the distribution in Kayes with FY 2012 funds (to be delivered in October 2013), and World Vision will provide sufficient LLINs to cover the region of Koulikoro. Global Fund's consolidated grant will procure LLINs to cover the needs for Bamako (1.15 million nets), which will complete this campaign cycle.

With the delay in the Global Fund grant signature, routine distribution channels encountered stockouts and PMI authorized the contribution of 600,000 LLINs initially planned for universal coverage campaigns to cover five months of routine distribution. PMI will continue to support the routine channels, and 1.2 million nets from FY 2012 will be distributed through the routine system. In 2014, PMI will use the 2 million nets procured with FY 2013 funds to conduct a mass campaign in Sikasso to replace the nets distributed in 2011.

Challenges, Opportunities, and Threats

- Despite high ownership and use rates in the highest risk populations, the surprisingly high parasitemia and anemia rates found in 2012 DHS raise questions about net effectiveness. Effectiveness may be compromised by poor net condition or insecticide retention or resistance to the pyrethroid insecticide used on LLINs. In addition, mosquito behavior and human behavior may further compromise the effectiveness of nets in some parts of Mali. PMI-supported research on the effectiveness of LLINs treated with insecticide plus a synergist on malaria transmission and parasite prevalence may help inform national policy on the type of LLIN to procure.

- Support has continued for improving coordination of BCC activities among PMI and NMCP partners to ensure uniform messaging on promoting correct and consistent LLIN use throughout the year. The PMI-funded Culture of Net Use Study was conducted in October 2012 to better understand how people use, care for, and repair mosquito nets , with the aim of informing a new national LLIN communication strategy. The study covered 40 households and 151 sleeping spaces in Kayes (no campaign) and Sikasso (campaign) Regions. The study confirmed high coverage of nets per sleeping space, willingness to purchase nets, and a generally high value placed on nets. Results of the study will be useful in developing better messaging for those who still do not use nets, encouraging net repair, and communicating information on proper washing. The results are also expected to describe the differences between populations that received a campaign net and those that had not.

Gap Analysis

The NMCP's gap analysis prepared by all key malaria partners in February 2013 notes the following number of nets available or committed for mass campaign and routine distribution by the MOH and partners:

LLIN gap analysis for campaigns, 2012-2015

Regions scheduled	2012 Segou and 2 districts in Kayes & Koulikoro and 3 northern regions	2013 Mopti and remaining Kayes	2014 Sikasso (round 2) and remaining Koulikoro	2015 Bamako, Gao, Tombouctou, Kidal plus Segou (round 2)
Population of scheduled region	4,569,980	4,442,592	5,824,564	6,785,025
Expected procurements				
PMI	2,300,000	2,400,000	1,400,000	1,400,000
UNICEF	70,000	0	0	0
Global Fund mass campaign		0	900,000	2,481,937
World Vision – 2012 covered 2 districts in Koulikoro	422,800	0	0	0
GOM (Mass campaign)			500,000	400,000
Total LLINs available	**2,792,800**	**2,400,000**	**2,800,000**	**4,281,937**
Total LLINs needed	**2,538,878**	**2,468,107**	**3,235,869**	**3,769,458**
Total gap (-) / surplus (+)	+253,922	-68,107	-435,869	+512,479

Mali's continued rolling campaign started in 2011 in Sikasso Region, covered Segou and two districts in Koulikoro and Kayes in early 2012, and Mopti Region in 2013 (except for two districts for security reasons). Kayes Region will be completed with 1.2 million nets in late 2013. Replacement of old nets with a new campaign will start in Sikasso Region in 2014 with 1.4 million nets. In 2015 the campaign will take place in the district of Bamako, the three northern regions of Gao, Tombouctou, and Kidal and the region of Segou for its second round. To ensure

26

one net for every 1.8 persons and assuming existing nets older than 3 years are not counted, a total of 3,769,458 nets will be needed. With the contributions from PMI in FY 2014 (1.4 million nets), the Global Fund (2,481,937), and GOM (400,000), there will be a surplus of 512,479 nets. But with the uncertainty of acquiring government nets, PMI will keep its contribution level at 1.4 million nets.

LLIN gap analysis for routine distribution, 2015

Total population, 2015	17,949,017
Pregnant women	897,451
Children under one year of age	717,971
Total LLINs needed	**1,615,442**
Expected procurements:	
PMI	600,000
Global Fund	959,278
GOM	100,000
Total LLINs available	**1,659,278**
Surplus	+43,856

For a population of 17,949,017 in 2015, the country will require 1,615,442 nets for routine distribution to pregnant women and fully immunized children under one year of age. All routine net needs are expected to be covered through planned procurements from the Global Fund, PMI, and the GOM, and a surplus of 43,856 nets will remain. Due to the uncertainty of the availability of GOM nets, PMI will maintain its level of contribution. If all donors honor their commitments, the surplus will be transferred to the continued rolling campaign.

Plans and Justification

PMI will continue its strong support of Mali's universal coverage strategies through both mass campaigns and routine services. The study of combination-insecticide-treated nets will begin in 2013 (with FY 2012 Funds) and will be completed before FY 2014 MOP activities are implemented. The PMI-supported study will help inform future national LLIN strategies in Mali.

Planned activities with FY 2014 funding ($8,525,000)

LLIN procurement: PMI will procure 2 million LLINs to support the NMCP's universal coverage objectives. Of the total contribution, 1,400,000 nets will help launch the 2015 mass campaign cycle in Segou Region, and 600,000 nets will be provided to children under one year of age and pregnant women through routine services nationwide. ($7,000,000)

Distribution of LLINs: PMI will support the distribution and follow-up of free LLINs through the mass campaign in Segou Region and through routine ANC and immunization services at the CSCOM level for infants and pregnant women. This support will include efforts to improve LLIN supply management, tracking, and forecasting routine LLIN distribution. ($1,500,000)

LLIN logistics strengthening: In parallel to other logistics strengthening efforts, PMI will provide resources for the NMCP to improve its own LLIN logistics management capacity, focusing on net tracking, coordination of donor inputs, and improving delivery systems from the district to CSCOM levels. ($25,000)

INDOOR RESIDUAL SPRAYING

NMCP/PMI Objectives

The NMCP's strategic plan envisions an integrated vector control program that includes LLINs, IRS, destruction of larval habitats, larviciding, and environmental management in urban zones. The NMCP considers IRS to be most effective in areas of the country where malaria transmission is perennial and has seasonal peaks that vary in duration from three to six months. The three northern regions of the country, as well as the northernmost districts within the Kayes, Koulikoro, Segou and Mopti Regions, which are considered areas of sporadic or epidemic-prone transmission, are not included in the IRS target area. IRS is also not ideal for rice-growing areas and zones of irrigation around the Niger River Delta where transmission is holoendemic, or in the urban areas of Bamako and Mopti, where much lower transmission occurs. PMI has continuously supported spraying in initially two, now three contiguous districts (Bla, Baraoueli, and Koulikoro) based on eco-epidemiological considerations (Figure 3) and also to act as the nucleus for future IRS districts. While no other partners are supporting large-scale IRS at the present time, private mining companies conduct IRS regularly in villages located within a 15-km radius of their mining sites. AngloGold, in Sadiola and Yatela mines, uses Actellic 50EC (an organophosphate class insecticide). Rand Gold Resources uses a carbamate insecticide (to be replaced with an organophosphate pending evaluation of residual effects) in the mines of Loulou, Morila, and Gounkoto.

Routine surveillance of vector insecticide resistance as well as other indicators, such as vector taxonomy, density, and biting behavior, informs the NMCP's program decisions about operations and selection of insecticides. A vector control needs assessment funded by PMI, has updated the national vector control strategy, which includes IRS in the context of the WHO integrated vector management (IVM) strategy. A major recommendation, to build capacity by strengthening technical and infrastructure capability of the NMCP, is also a PMI objective. This will be achieved by strengthening the capacity of the NCMP and regional and district teams, in planning, implementing and monitoring IRS operations, and by supporting operation research by MRTC and other scientific/research entities in Mali to inform decisions regarding vector susceptibility/resistance.

PMI-supported IRS started by using pyrethroid insecticides during the three first years (2008-2010), and then following the appearance of resistance to pyrethroids in 2010, shifted to a carbamate insecticide.

28

Figure 3. IRS targets three districts, Bla, Baroueli and Koulikoro, in the North Sudanese ecological zone

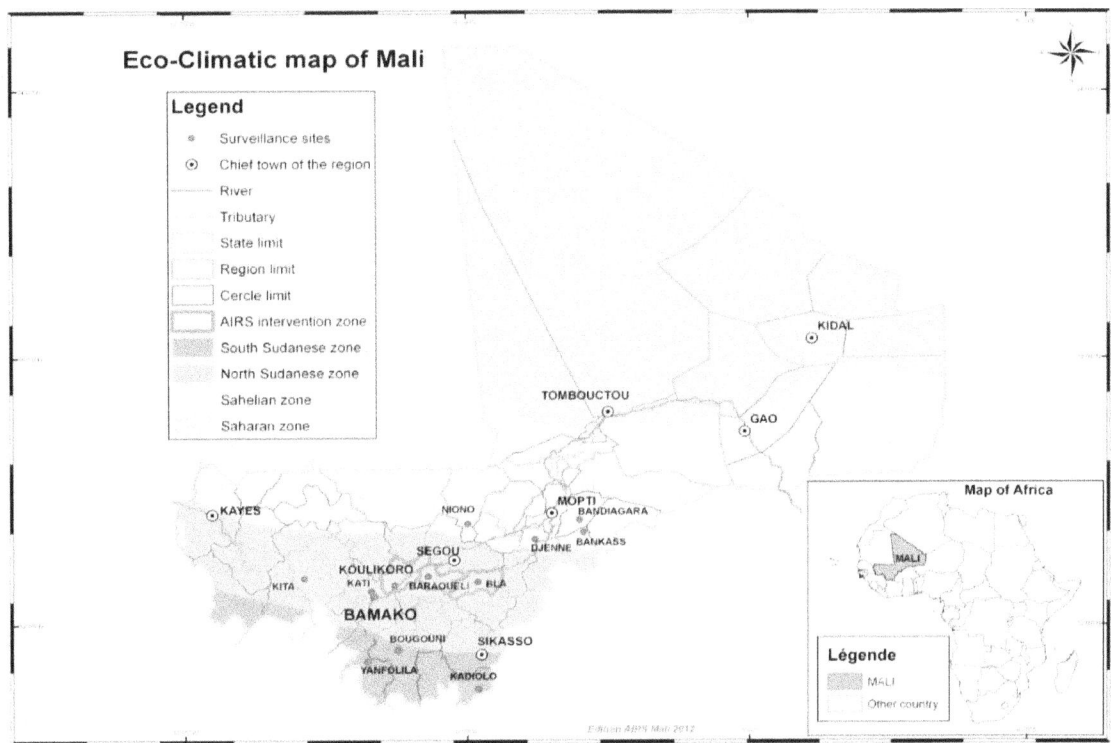

Table 1. Types of malaria transmission in Mali and geographic areas

Transmission type	Geographic areas	Seasonality; level
Endemic, perennial	South Sudanese zone	
Endemic, seasonal (long)	North Sudanese and Sahelian zones Bamako, Mopti	Seasonal peak (June-November) Lower than surrounding area
Endemic, perennial	Niger River Delta, areas near dams and rice cultivation; urban areas	Low level
Endemic, seasonal (short)	North-central Sahelian zone	Seasonal peak (July-October)
Epidemic	North Saharan Zone, including Tombouctou, Gao, and Kidal;	

Progress during the last 12 months

IRS coverage was nearly doubled in 2011 by expanding to include a third district, Baroueli. The IRS strategy calls for IRS to expand outward from this nucleus, eventually covering the North Sudanese and Sahelian zones. However, it is recognized that additional IRS partners will be necessary to meet this objective.

The March 2012 *coup* that led to the suspension of USG assistance to the GoM negatively impacted the preparation of the 2012 IRS program. The project was temporarily suspended and when reauthorized to restart work, it was not allowed to work with the GoM and MRTC (also temporarily suspended), which was in charge of entomological monitoring of IRS in the previous spray rounds. To address this situation, the IRS project set up a strong entomological team that was able to build an insectary in a container box and carry out entomological monitoring activities.

The IRS round in 2012 targeted structures in Koulikoro, Bla, and Baroueli Districts, using carbamates. The round sprayed 206,295 structures and protected 762,147 people, including 18,561 pregnant women and 145,953 children under five years of age. In addition, 769 supervisors and spray operators were trained, and 1,172 community volunteers were trained.

PMI-supported IRS spray rounds, 2008-2012

Date	Insecticide (class)	Target districts	Structures sprayed	Population protected
July - August 2008	λ-cyhalothrin (pyrethroid)	Bla Koulikoro	108,000	420,580
May - July 2009	λ-cyhalothrin (pyrethroid)	Bla Koulikoro	127,000	497,122
May - June 2010	deltamethrin (pyrethroid)	Bla Koulikoro	127,000	441,000
June - July 2011	bendiocarb (carbamate)	Bla Koulikoro Baroueli	203,000	700,000
July – August 2012	bendiocarb (carbamate)	Bla Koulikoro Baroueli	206,295	762,147
August – September 2013 (planned)	bendiocarb (carbamate)	Bla Koulikoro Baroueli	Estimated 210,000	Estimated 760,000

Insecticide susceptibility data (Figures 4 and 5) were collected at thirteen randomly selected and nationally representative sentinel sites: the three IRS target districts and ten additional locations (see Figure 3) for regional susceptibility mapping. These data informed the decision to continue

IRS with a carbamate-class insecticide for the 2013 IRS spray round. The IRS entomologic monitoring and evaluation activity documented complete susceptibility to organo-phosphate class insecticides, and a rotation to this class may occur in 2014, depending on the 2013 post-IRS insecticide susceptibility test results and residual efficacy data. Reduced susceptibility to pyrethroid insecticides remains widespread, which is a potential concern because LLINs are treated with pyrethroids. In summary, current data indicate complete insecticide susceptibility to organophosphate insecticides and carbamate insecticides (except for one site in Kita District, where possible emerging resistance to carbamate was observed).

Figure 4. *An. gambiae s.l.* susceptibility to carbamates, 13 sites, 2012

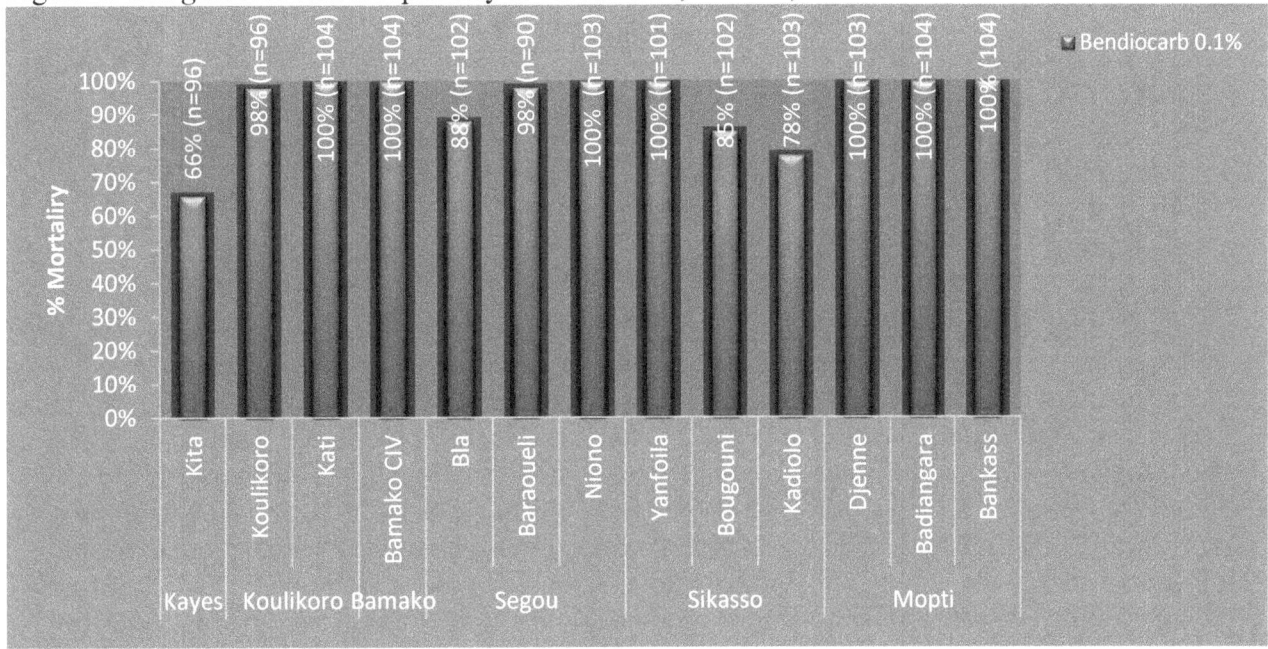

Figure 5. 2012 *An. gambiae s.l.* susceptibility to pyrethroids at 13 sites, 2012

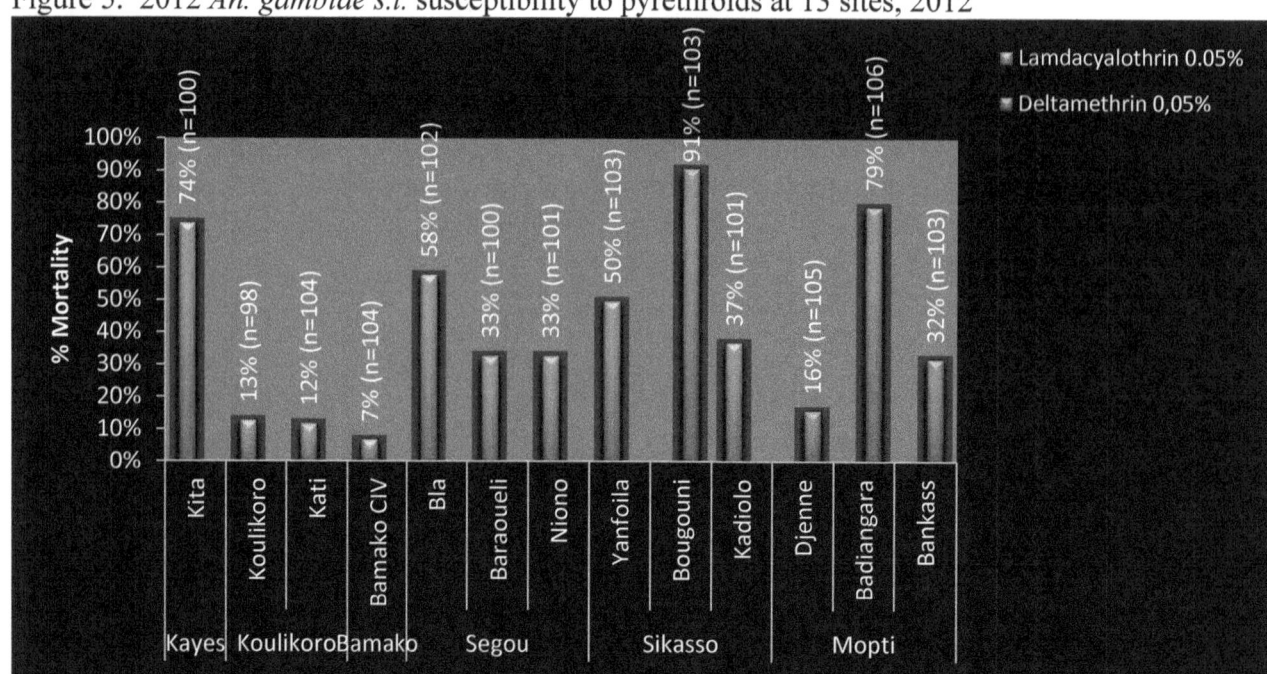

PMI-supported entomological monitoring confirmed a second issue related to the use of carbamate insecticides: their residual effect is relatively short compared to the duration of the transmission season). The observed changes in vector density before and after IRS (Figure 6) indicate that carbamate effects degrade in approximately two months, a result which has also been confirmed by a third monitoring method, the WHO cone wall bioassay. At one month post-IRS, walls were fully insecticidal (>80% mosquito mortality following exposure) in seven of eight locations in the IRS zone. However, at three months, results indicated that the IRS residual effect had failed (<80% mosquito mortality) at all sites. In response to this problem, spraying in 2013 will be delayed until July-August (also done in 2012) in order to shift the limited insecticidal effect to the August/September high transmission period.

Entomologic and evaluation results (Figure 6) show the relatively short residual effect of IRS on mosquito density, as well as the decline in late transmission season (Oct-Nov) vector density (non-spray data). During the early transmission season (June-July), vector densities are generally lower as there is less standing water for breeding during the early rainy season. Therefore, by delaying IRS operations until July, it is possible to partially compensate for the short-acting residual effect of the insecticide.

Figure 6. IRS entomological monitoring and evaluation results, by zone, 2012.

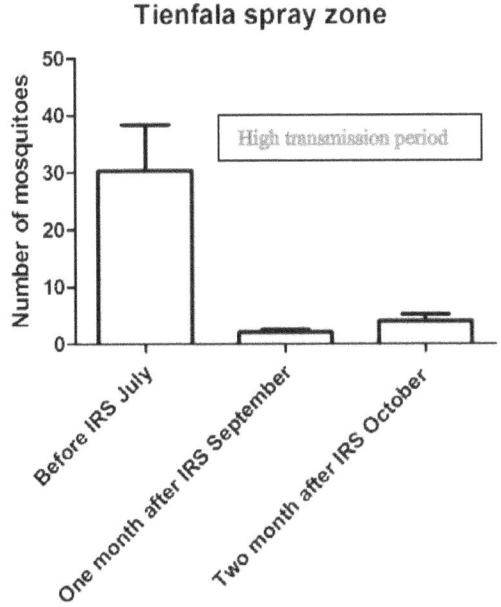

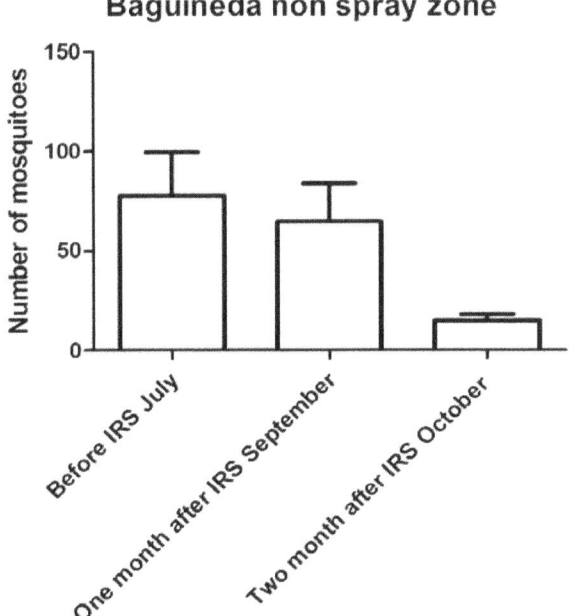

Challenges, Opportunities, and Threats

- A technical challenge is to extend the residual effect of IRS to cover the entire transmission season. In addition to well-timed deployment of IRS, careful selection of the IRS insecticide class and rotation strategies to mitigate resistance-related loss of impact will play a central role in future IRS planning. Use of an organophosphate insecticide (a long-lasting CS formulation) may be considered for the 2014 IRS round based on FY 2013 IRS residual efficacy data.

- Programmatically, the challenge is to operationalize Mali's IVM strategy to manage IRS resources and to attract additional IRS partners.

- Significant entomological capacity exists in Mali and the country has the potential to develop its own IRS program. To do this, the NMCP and its IRS partners must leverage existing strengths and identify adequate financial resources. Capacity building may take the form of private sector partnerships (e.g., mining companies) to extend IRS spraying activities outward. Additional resources to expand IRS may come as a result of the IVM strategy to align approaches and efforts of multiple donors into one concerted push.

Plans and Justification

With FY 2014 funding, PMI proposes continued support to the NMCP's IRS strategy, based on the IVM approach. Three districts will be targeted for one round of IRS, including support for training, supervision, communications, and operations. To address technical challenges, e.g.

vector insecticide resistance and effective life of the insecticide, PMI will continue to support IRS/entomological monitoring to inform program decisions. PMI will continue its support for vector collection and testing at the 13 entomological surveillance locations. Additionally, PMI will support transfer and use of new vector-insecticide susceptibility testing methods to identify mechanisms of vector insecticide resistance, as well as distribution and levels of phenotypic resistance. Assuming the July 2013 elections occur, PMI will be in a position to fully engage with the NMCP in the important work of building capacity, identifying additional partners to support an IRS expansion based on past experience and promoting IVM strategies for vector control.

Planned activities with FY 2014 funding ($5,484,000)

IRS implementation: PMI will support one round of IRS in three target districts to spray approximately 210,000 structures. Insecticide resistance patterns, assessed following the 2013 IRS round, will be used to inform the choice of insecticide. PMI will procure the necessary quantities of insecticide to cover the three districts, but reduction in geographic coverage may be considered if the insecticide choice changes to an organophosphate insecticide. However, with FY 2013 funds PMI will support the NMCP to develop a comprehensive IRS national strategy document that will be used as an advocacy tool to seek funding from other donors. PMI will procure spray pumps and personal protective equipment and will support all the operational costs including selection, training, and supervision of spray operators and environmental compliance. Communications efforts to promote acceptance and compliance with IRS will precede the spray round. ($5,100,000)

Technical assistance for vector control activities: An entomologist from the Centers for Disease Control and Prevention (CDC) will conduct two technical assistance visits: one to assist the PMI entomology monitoring partner to evaluate IRS insecticidal activity and to support operations research on dual-insecticide LLINs (vector collections to be managed by IRS partner); and a second trip to design and supervise expanded entomological surveillance to evaluate vector insecticide resistance using CDC testing methods. ($24,000)

Entomological monitoring: PMI will support two activities: (1) Annual vector insecticide susceptibility monitoring at thirteen sentinel sites to inform selection of IRS insecticides and to map trends in vector susceptibility; evaluate the impact of resistance management strategies and of combined IRS and LLIN activities; and (2) Conducting IRS-related entomologic assessments at ten sites: six in IRS districts (two per district) plus four non-IRS (comparison) sites. This will include capacity building in entomological monitoring of IRS for the NMCP entomologist and the Division of Hygiene and Sanitation within the National Directorate of Health. ($360,000)

MALARIA IN PREGNANCY

NMCP/PMI Objectives

Mali's malaria in pregnancy (MIP) strategy applies WHO's three-pronged approach: providing three doses of IPTp with SP, promoting the use of LLINs distributed free at the first ANC visit, and effective case management of suspected malarial illnesses. The NMCP has set ambitious goals for MIP through the National Strategic Plan. The program aims to provide 100% of pregnant women living in stable transmission zones three doses of SP for IPTp at ANC services as per the national guidelines. The NMCP also has a goal of universal coverage with LLINs and, as part of that policy, intends to provide bed nets to 100% of pregnant women through ANC clinics, as a supplement to the mass campaign distribution. In 2006, the MOH issued directives ensuring free provision of SP for IPTp. In October 2012, WHO changed its recommendations for IPTp to administering a dose of SP at every ANC visit after quickening. Much of the original research behind this policy change occurred in Mali, so Mali became an early adopter of the new recommendations and revised the national policy in November 2012.

Utilization of ANC services by pregnant women is moderate but increasing. In 2001 only 57% of women attended ANC at least once. As of 2012, approximately 74% of women attended ANC at least once during their most recent pregnancy, according to the preliminary DHS findings. Current data on attendance patterns are not yet available; however, the 2006 DHS showed that ANC attendance usually occurs late, with only 30% of pregnant women attending before the end of their first trimester of pregnancy. IPTp use is low, as the 2012 DHS showed that only 20% of women received two doses of SP at ANC visits (up from 4% in the 2006 DHS). Health facilities also collect and report information quarterly through the national SLIS on the number of ANC visits (including early ANC visits), postnatal consultations, SP doses administered, and assisted deliveries by a skilled birth attendant. In 2007, the MOH released revised ANC visit cards that included IPTp and LLIN information. The 2012 SLIS showed 47% of pregnant women attending one ANC visit obtained one dose and 32% received two doses of SP. Because of the political situation, the SLIS was not complete. The use of bed nets in general is very high in Mali and preliminary data from the DHS 2012 show that approximately 75% of pregnant women slept under an ITN the night before the survey.

For case management in pregnancy, the national policy is to use quinine in the first trimester and the first line ACT (AL) in the second and third trimesters. Treatment of severe malaria follows the same protocols as with nonpregnant adults: quinine, or injectable artesunate if available. Details on PMI's support to the overall case management program, including drug procurement and supply chain issues, are available in the case management section of this MOP.

Integration and coordination between the NMCP and the MOH's Reproductive Health Unit is critical in ensuring effective MIP programs and high IPTp coverage. Since 2006, the NMCP and the Reproductive Health Unit have developed a revised in-service training module for focused antenatal care (FANC), which includes MIP and IPTp.

The National Center for Information, Education, and Communication for Health (*Centre National d'Information Education et Communication pour la Santé*), which is tasked with creating BCC materials and strategies, is addressing barriers to increasing uptake of IPTp by improving providers' interpersonal communication skills and encouraging early ANC visits by pregnant women.

Progress during the last 12 months

To explore the reasons for the low uptake of IPTp in Mali, PMI supported an assessment of the barriers to implementation of IPTp in ANC clinics. The assessment indicated that, in general, women knew about IPTp and had favorable opinions about taking SP to prevent complications of MIP. At the same time, the assessment highlighted a number of misconceptions regarding IPTp on the part of both providers and pregnant women. Among the findings was the pervasive belief that SP cannot be taken on an empty stomach, nor can it be taken after the 7th or 8th month of pregnancy. The most recent policy recommendations from WHO address many of these issues directly, but these barriers still need to be addressed in many parts of Mali. The assessment report was finalized in early 2012 and the findings are being incorporated into provider training activities in order to dispel outdated concepts around IPTp delivery.

PMI has supported in-service training and supervision of health providers, in collaboration with the Reproductive Health Unit, NMCP, and Midwives Association to facilitate the implementation of the MIP guidelines as well as the training of health providers on interpersonal communication, an area cited by the MOH as a challenge. Due to the political unrest in Mali, PMI's implementing partners were unable to carry out activities for several months in 2012. Nonetheless, when the suspension was lifted for PMI's principal health service delivery project at the end of October 2012, the project immediately restarted its training program. From October 2012 through March 2013, 159 trainers and providers were trained in FANC, including the implementation of IPTp. These trainings included dissemination of policy guidelines and job aids to assist health care workers in the provision of services.

Other PMI-supported partners have promoted the provision of free LLINs to pregnant women at their first ANC visit; in practice, LLINs are often not given until the third or fourth ANC visit. PMI supported a multi-channel BCC strategy targeting pregnant women, women of childbearing age, and men, focusing on knowledge and perceptions related to MIP, women's awareness of risks of malaria during pregnancy, early and frequent ANC attendance at health facility, early use of IPTp in the second trimester, completion of the recommended two treatment courses of IPTp, provision of a free LLIN at the first ANC visit, and increasing demand for proper treatment of MIP.

Challenges, Opportunities, and Threats

- A considerable barrier to IPTp in Mali arises from pregnant women having to pay for antenatal care. In 2006, the MOH announced that IPTp would be provided free; however, women are required to pay for the ANC card (which allows them access to a basic package of services). Women also report that they are still required to pay for all other medicines prescribed by clinicians, and consultation fees remain prohibitively high. Advocacy for removal of consultation fees has been ongoing at the central level.

- Beyond the political concerns, there are programmatic challenges to MIP interventions in Mali that are not dissimilar to those encountered in other countries. Both providers and community members misunderstand the importance of preventing MIP and what steps they can take to do so. PMI has planned a strong program of training for providers to reinforce the message that MIP activities are integral to the FANC approach that WHO recommends.

- In the past, Mali experienced stockouts of SP due to procurement and supply chain management issues. In April 2011, the end use verification survey found that 85% of health facilities were stocked out of SP. Subsequently, PMI has undertaken to fund the procurement of enough SP to cover the anticipated needs for 2012 and 2013. The survey in September 2012 found that 28% of facilities remain stocked out of SP. PMI will continue to procure 100% of the national need for SP in 2014 and is working very closely with local authorities and implementing partners to address supply chain issues.

Gap Analysis

PMI will support the NMCP objective of 100% coverage of all pregnant women in accordance with the new WHO recommendations. The NMCP conducted a gap analysis, based on an early dosing regimen, which resulted in a request for 1.8 million doses of SP for 2015. After reviewing the calculations, and taking into account actual attendance patterns at ANC, the team agreed to procure this quantity of SP, which was deemed sufficient for FY 2014 needs. At the same time, PMI is working on a number of fronts to increase ANC utilization and, if routine monitoring indicates an increased need for SP, PMI will procure additional doses as needed. Currently neither the MOH nor other donors have committed to purchasing SP to cover the annual IPTp needs.

Plans and Justification

PMI will support the NMCP and MOH with its multipronged approach to MIP, including contributing to annual MIP commodity needs (LLINs and SP), improving facility-level FANC services and health provider practices through training and supervision, and promoting coverage of MIP interventions through community mobilization and BCC messages. PMI will support the revision and dissemination of revised guidelines on IPTp and folic acid use in accordance with WHO recommendations. PMI will support early and frequent attendance of pregnant women at ANCs, and work with the MOH and other donors to ensure SP is available, used correctly, and provided free to pregnant women for IPTp. Through training of health providers in FANC to address barriers to implementation of IPTp and strengthening of the commodity system, PMI will continue to improve MIP services and increase IPTp rates. PMI will also support engagement and mobilization of pregnant women and the promotion of MIP services at the community level through traditional leaders, midwives, and coordinated and harmonized BCC activities.

Planned activities with FY 2014 funding ($795,000)

SP Procurement: PMI will procure 1.8 million SP treatments to contribute to covering the annual need for the estimated 900,000 pregnant women attending ANC in 2015, including handling and distribution costs. To increase uptake of IPTp directly-observed therapy, PMI will provide 250 health centers with sufficient water filters and cups so that IPTp can be taken with clean water at the facility. ($270,000)

Strengthen MIP/FANC at facility level: PMI will work with the NMCP and partners to roll out updated national guidelines that correspond with WHO's revised recommendations for IPTp administration at every ANC visit after the first trimester. PMI will support training of health providers to provide quality services to pregnant women at ANC visits including ensuring the provision of free SP for IPTp. PMI will work with partners, including the MOH Reproductive Health Division and the Midwives Association, to expand use of the in-service FANC training module and increase supportive supervision during IPTp implementation nationally through facility and community outreach activities. ($525,000)

CASE MANAGEMENT

Diagnostics

NMCP/PMI Objectives

Mali's case management policy is in line with WHO guidelines requiring that every malaria case should be laboratory confirmed before administering ACTs and that where microscopy is not available, RDTs should be used to confirm the diagnosis. Microscopic diagnosis is performed in 4 national, 6 regional, and 60 district hospitals at a cost ranging between $0.75-$5 per blood smear. In addition to hospitals' providing microscopy, some privately operated CSCOMs staffed with physicians and/or laboratory technicians also perform malaria microscopy. Most CSCOMs do not have the capacity to do microscopy and rely on RDTs for malaria diagnosis. The RDTs are provided free of charge to children less than five years of age and pregnant women and highly subsidized for other groups. The National Institute of Public Health Research (*The Institut National de Recherche en Santé Publique* [INRSP]) is responsible for QC of all diagnostic services. With PMI funding, the institute has developed and finalized a QA/QC plan for malaria microscopy and RDTs. However, implementation of the plan was suspended after the military *coup*.

Progress during the last 12 months

With FY 2012 funding, PMI procured more than 2 million RDTs and supported initial training on malaria RDTs for 156 health workers in the Kignan District of the Sikasso Region. A recent national health facility survey carried out in 2012 at 57 facilities in Mali found that 91% of CSCOMs and 94% of CSREFs had at least one staff member trained in RDTs, and that 24% of CSCOMs and 100% of CSREFs had at least one staff member trained in malaria microscopy. According to the end-use verification assessment conducted in August–September 2012, 77% of facilities surveyed had RDTs in stock on the day of the team's visit.

Diagnostic confirmation of suspected malaria cases has increased substantially in the last few years: routine data show that 18% of suspected malaria cases were tested by microscopy or RDT in 2010, increasing to 32% in 2011 and 52% in 2012. The 2012 health facility survey similarly found that about half of suspected malaria cases were diagnostically confirmed: 63% of children under five years with suspected malaria were tested with either microscopy or RDT, while 47% of over-five patients with suspected malaria were tested at these facilities.

Challenges, Opportunities, and Threats

- Though access to quality diagnostics is a problem throughout Mali especially in rural areas, it is now particularly difficult in the north due to insecurity. Providing commodities, training, and supervision will be a challenge. The program will have to rely on multilateral agencies with access to the north to assist with delivering diagnostic and other services.

- Due to suspension of PMI activities after the military *coup* in March 2012, PMI's initial and refresher activities on diagnostics were suspended for many months, resulting in many fewer health workers trained in malaria diagnostics than planned. Initial training of health workers who had not been trained previously on malaria diagnostics was prioritized.

- The INRSP has recently finalized a QA/QC plan for laboratory services and all diagnostics, but suspended funding has halted implementation of this plan and supervision of malaria diagnostics performance at health facilities.

Gap Analysis

In February 2013, malaria stakeholders convened in Bamako to carry out a gap analysis of key malaria commodities, including diagnostics and ACTs. The Global Fund Round 10 grant, originally developed in 2009 but on hold due to fund mismanagement, has recently been signed. The Global Fund will provide RDTs and this will help prevent a previously anticipated shortage in 2013 and 2014. It is anticipated that 100% of suspected malaria cases seen in the community by CHWs will be confirmed by RDT and 80% of cases at health facilities will be confirmed by

RDT and the remaining 20% by microscopy. The Global Fund is planning to finance all microscopy needs in 2015.

RDT gap analysis, 2013-2015

	2013	**2014**	**2015**
Malaria tests required at health facilities and in the community	3,785,048	3,613,599	3,281,406
Coverage of diagnostic tests	100%	100%	100%
% covered by microscopy	10%	10%	10%
% covered by RDTs	90%	90%	90%
Number of microscopy tests required	378,505	361,360	328,141**
Number of RDTs required	**3,406,544**	**3,252,239**	**2,953,265**
RDTs covered by Global Fund (Round 10)	1,163,993	1,704,837	1,984,948
RDTs covered by PMI	2,000,000	1,500,000	1,500,000
Total RDTs planned	**3,163,993**	**3,204,837**	**3,484,948**
RDT gap (-)/surplus (+)	**-242,551**	**-47,402**	**+531,683**

*RDT needs based on a gap analysis led by Systems for Improved Access to Pharmaceuticals and Services in February 2013.
** Microscopy needs planned to be covered in entirety by the Global Fund.

Plans and Justification

To support the NMCP and sustain the trend of increasing malaria diagnostic confirmation, PMI will procure sufficient RDTs to contribute to the annual nationwide need. From the gap analysis, PMI plans to procure 1.5 million RDTs in FY 2014 to contribute to health facility and iCCM needs for the period of 2014-2015. A portion of these RDTs will be available for emergency and epidemic preparedness and response.

PMI will continue to support supervision and on-site training of health facility workers to improve the quality of malaria diagnostics. PMI will allocate funding for supportive supervision for laboratory technicians and clinicians so that INRSP's QA/QC plan for malaria diagnostics can be implemented. Staff from the NMCP will conduct joint supervision visits with INRSP staff to CSRef facilities and will work with CSRef staff to ensure they are adequately supervising CSCOM staff on malaria diagnostics (primarily RDTs).

Planned activities with FY 2014 funding ($1,362,000)

Procurement of RDTs: PMI will procure approximately 1.5 million RDTs to cover the remaining gap left after contributions from the Global Fund Round consolidated grant for

CSCOMs nationwide and to supply ASCs as part of the national iCCM strategy. This procurement also allows some room to fill potential gaps due to donor fluctuations and for epidemic response. ($1,000,000)

Quality assurance/quality control for diagnostics: In addition to in-service training, PMI will support the NMCP and INRSP to implement its recently finalized plan for QA/QC for microscopy and RDT diagnostics, including regular supervisory visits. A combination of observation of health worker performing RDTs, comparison of results of RDTs stored under optimal conditions at the reference laboratory with RDTs stored in the field, and comparison of RDTs against microscopy to check RDT performance will be used. The plan aims to train two technicians per CSRef or hospital for a total of approximately 146 microscopy technicians. The plan will also include QA/QC for the CSCOM and the CHW level as well to ensure good quality malaria diagnostics at all levels of the health system ($150,000)

Technical assistance on diagnostics: A CDC laboratory technician or epidemiologist will provide technical assistance to assist in implementation of the QA/QC plan throughout the health system down to the community level and recommend best practices for the plan's implementation. ($12,000)

Formative supervision of laboratory technicians and clinicians: PMI will continue to support supervision and on-site training of laboratory technicians and clinicians in malaria diagnostics. The focus of this training will be on microscopy, RDTs, quality of laboratory services, and adherence to test results at regional, district, and CSCOM levels. More than 2,057 health workers will be trained and supervised (with additional PMI support for this activity referenced in the case management section) ($200,000)

Treatment

NMCP/PMI Objectives

The MOH revised their national policy for the treatment of uncomplicated malaria to make AL the first-line drug in 2010. As per national directive, ACTs are free to children less than five years of age and pregnant women in the second and third trimesters. Three regimens are described in Mali's case management policy for severe malaria: intravenous quinine, injectable artemether, and injectable artesunate, though injectable quinine is still mentioned as the treatment of choice for severe malaria. Health centers typically use whatever severe malaria medication is available. The new 2013–2017 Malaria Strategic Plan notes that injectable artesunate should be the drug of choice for severe malaria, though quinine and injectable artemether can also be used. The Chinese government donated a large supply of injectable artesunate in 2011 but as of mid-2013 there has been no formal or systematic training on injectable artesunate for malaria case management. The manufacturer of the injectable artesunate put together a job aid that was distributed to health facilities in 2011 and has funded a cascade training activity on severe malaria that will be implemented in summer 2013. A 2012 national health facility survey found poor performance of health workers in terms of severe malaria case management, with more than 50% of patients receiving treatment for an incorrect number of days. With reprogrammed FY 2013 funding, PMI will fund an update of the malaria case management guidelines to recommend injectable artesunate as the treatment of choice and will include specific training on injectable artesunate, which PMI is procuring.

The NMCP and MRTC initiated supervision of malaria case management practices in 2010 starting with Bamako and transitioning to other regions. These visits cover district referral health centers (CSRefs), where the team provides training of trainers to district health leads to provide supervisory support in their specific district. The team uses supervisory tools developed in collaboration with NMCP, PMI, MRTC, and malaria partners to focus on the proportion of suspected malaria cases tested, adherence to test results when prescribing ACTs, and improving care of patients with severe febrile disease. Malaria supervision guidelines were updated in February 2012 and include supervision of outpatient consultations at health facilities, antenatal consultations, and CHW visits.

Poor geographic and economic access to care is a major challenge for malaria treatment in Mali. With approximately 1,134 CSCOMs in the country in 2012, about 83% of the population has geographic access to public health services according to WHO standards (living within 15 km of a first-line health facility) but only 54% live within 5 km of a health facility. All patients must pay consultation fees and patients five years and older must pay fees for malaria diagnostics and drugs, though these are subsidized. A health financing task force has been set up to examine issues related to user fees for primary care in Mali, a complex issue with a long history dating back to the Bamako Initiative in 1987 that set up revolving drug funds at CSCOMs.

The 2012 DHS showed that only 26% of children less than five years of age with fever received any antimalarial, and only 21% were treated the same day or the day following symptom onset. A PMI-supported national health facility assessment in 2012 found good availability of ACTs at health facilities, with 92% of facilities surveyed having ACTs in stock. The survey revealed that 61% of health workers reported receiving formal training in ACTs and 60% received information training in ACT use. Health workers generally prescribed ACTs in correct doses but suspected cases of malaria were not systematically tested, with only 63% of suspected cases in children less than five years of age receiving a malaria test and only 47% of those five and older tested. The September 2012 end use verification survey found that most patients with simple malaria were treated correctly with an ACT, but 14% were treated incorrectly, primarily with injectable quinine.

To overcome barriers of access to health services, the MOH adopted an integrated community case management (iCCM) package in February 2010 that includes treatment for malaria, diarrhea, pneumonia and malnutrition, essential newborn care, and family planning. Free treatment for children under five is provided by trained ASCs (though patients must pay a consultation fee) and includes malaria diagnosis with RDTs and treatment with ACTs, although diarrhea and pneumonia medications are not free. Severe cases are referred to CSCOMs.

The private health sector also plays a sizeable role in Mali, particularly in urban areas, where private pharmacies and clinical practices are more common. Relatively little is known about malaria care in the private sector. The NMCP would like to work more closely with the private sector to ensure providers are following correct treatment guidelines and reporting on malaria cases. As an initial step, PMI and the Mission are supporting a mapping exercise of all pharmaceutical structures (private and governmental) to develop a list or registry of the sector for regulatory and planning purposes. Based on the outcome of this exercise, PMI will determine how best to move forward with strengthening private sector case management practices including diagnostics. An initial activity may include conducting a more comprehensive assessment of private provider practices, followed by a targeted training to improve malaria case management and reporting.

In the new 2013–2017 Malaria Strategic Plan, Mali introduced SMC with four rounds of SP and amodiaquine for children under five years of age as a key malaria control intervention. Following a successful pilot of SMC in Koutiala District (in the Kayes Region) in 2012, which showed a 42% reduction in malaria cases , the NMCP has developed a plan to implement SMC in all districts of Mali, although scale-up will depend on donor funds and may likely be piecemeal. Although the NMCP plans to scale up SMC nationwide, it is worth noting that not all regions of Mali meet the WHO criteria for being appropriate for SMC (>60% of rainfall within three months and malaria incidence > 0.1 clinical episodes per year among children ages 3–59 months). The three northern regions of the country are not appropriate for SMC, but the vast majority of Mali, including the areas PMI will support, meet the WHO criteria for SMC.

Progress during the last 12 months

With FY 2012 funding, PMI procured 2 million ACT treatments for health facilities and ASCs implementing iCCM. PMI supported initial training on malaria case management with ACTs for 234 health workers in the Kignan District of Sikasso Region in 2012, where health workers had not previously received initial training. Although PMI financing for supervision activities was halted for several months, the 2012 national health facility survey found that 61% of health workers reported having received formal training on ACTs and 60% received informal training in ACT use.

To date, PMI has supported implementation of iCCM in five health districts of Sikasso Region and in two districts each in Kayes and Ségou Regions. From January 2012 to March 2013, PMI-supported partners have treated 54,967 malaria cases at the community level with trained ASCs in the seven districts in Sikasso and Kayes. In addition to USAID, UNICEF, and CIDA are key partners in funding iCCM in Mali. As of May 2013, a total of 2,213 ASCs had been trained in the full iCCM package and deployed in five of Mali's eight regions.

Challenges, Opportunities, and Threats

- After the military *coup* in March 2012, PMI's initial and refresher activities on diagnostics were suspended for many months, resulting in many fewer health workers trained in malaria case management than planned. Prior to the suspension of activities, initial training of health workers who had not been trained previously on malaria case management was prioritized, but refresher training was not carried out as planned.

- Although the MOH has officially adopted iCCM, mobilizing the resources to support large-scale implementation will remain a challenge in case management even thoughsupport is shared by several donors. The five-year Global Round 10 signed in

May 2013 will support 50% of the ASCs' salaries; a mix of local government and other donor funding will be needed to continue to support the remaining 50%. UNICEF has submitted a proposal to CIDA and the French government for supporting this, and the local government in Sikasso is planning to support 50% of ASCs' salary in their region. ASCs also face challenges in terms of RDT and ACT availability and regular supervision.

- Financial accessibility remains one of the largest challenges to prompt care-seeking for malaria. Patients, including those under five years of age, must pay a consultation fee for care with ASCs and at CSCOMs. Malaria diagnostics and drugs are free for children under five years, but patients five years and older must still pay a fee for these commodities, though they are highly subsidized.

- Delays in procuring SP and amodiaquine for implementation of SMC have delayed implementation of SMC. PMI decided to postpone until 2014 the planned implementation in Kita District in July 2013 as the drugs were not expected to arrive in time. UNICEF is funding SP and amodiaquine for seven districts, but it is unclear whether drugs will arrive in time to implement SMC in 2013.

Gap Analysis

In February 2013, malaria stakeholders in Mali, including the NMCP, Global Fund, PMI, and others met to conduct a quantification exercise for malaria commodities. Based on this exercise, the group determined needs and commitment for ACTs. Funding for ACTs will be provided by the Global Fund and PMI. The exercise did not include quantification of drugs for severe malaria. The number of cases of severe malaria reported in the SLIS in 2012 was 646,388. However, these cases were not systematically confirmed with malaria diagnostics and likely represent an overestimate of the true number of cases of severe malaria. No other donors have committed to funding drugs for severe malaria.

ACT gap analysis, 2013-2015

	2013	2014	2015
Number of cases of uncomplicated malaria	**2,763,086**	**2,637,928**	**2,395,426**
Proportion of cases treated at:			
Health centers	74%	71%	70%
Community level	26%	29%	30%
Private sector	0	0	0
Number of cases at:			
Health centers	2,048,324	1,860,484	1,676,798
Community level	714,762	777,444	718,628
Private sector	0	0	0
ACT Needs by AL dose			
AL 1 x 6	854,618	881,885	806,503
AL 2 x 6	624,105	654,396	599,287
AL 3 x 6	450,739	886,615	347,307
AL 4 x 6	833,624	715,031	642,330
ACTs covered by Global Fund	981,979	1,410,994	1,622,540
ACTs covered by PMI	1,200,000	1,200,000	1,200,000
Total ACTs covered	**2,181,979**	**2,610,994**	**2,822,540**
Gap (-) or Surplus (+)	**-581,107**	**-26,934**	**+427,114**

* ACT needs for facility and iCCM are based gap analysis exercise led by SIAPs in February 2013 with input from malaria partners.

Plans and Justification

With FY 2014 funding, PMI will continue to procure ACTs for malaria case management at health facility and community levels. In addition, PMI will procure sufficient quantities of injectable artesunate for meeting the severe malaria treatment needs nationally. In light of the suspension of training and supervision for several months in 2012, PMI will prioritize training and supervision for malaria case management, especially around severe malaria to address deficiencies found in this area. PMI will continue to support the NMCP's conducting formative supervision visits to assess the use of AL and artesunate.

PMI will support implementation of the full package of iCCM in three regions: Sikasso, Kayes, and Koulikoro, including support for training and supervision. PMI will also support implementation of SMC in three districts in these regions. Finally, PMI funding will support a pilot of improving malaria case management in the private sector.

Planned activities with FY 2014 funding ($5,189,000)

Treatment for uncomplicated malaria: PMI will procure 1.2 million AL treatments to contribute towards treatment needs at health facilities and for iCCM. ($1,724,000)

Treatment for severe malaria: PMI will procure 300,000 treatment packs of injectable artesunate for treatment of patients with severe malaria at CSRef (and selected CSCOM) levels. This contribution represents approximately half of the annual need based on more than 646,000 severe malaria cases reported in 2012. ($735,000)

Training and supervision for malaria case management: After training health personnel at all levels in case management, PMI will continue to support the NMCP to conduct quarterly supervisory visits in order to maintain and strengthen the quality of services at multiple levels of the health delivery system. Particular emphasis will be placed on training and supervision for severe malaria case management. PMI is supporting several partners to provide diagnosis and case management support to the NMCP at national, regional, district and community levels. Both supervision and training on diagnosis and case management are provided in an integrated fashion, targeting about 1,620 out of 4,300 health workers nationwide. ($450,000)

iCCM implementation: PMI will support iCCM implementation in all districts in Sikasso, Kayes, and Koulikoro Regions; while other donors, including UNICEF, Global Fund as well as the GOM, will provide support for iCCM activities in the other targeted regions. PMI support for iCCM includes continued support to the malaria/fever component of the iCCM package, with new and refresher trainings at district levels, supportive supervision, training in appropriate RDT use, evaluating ASC performance with RDTs, monitoring and evaluation, and provision of ASC materials and supplies. PMI will support ASCs to provide appropriate health communications and BCC messages to encourage understanding and adherence to current treatment algorithms. PMI will continue to support the NMCP to coordinate all community health implementing partners to ensure that community health materials (e.g., training modules, job aids, motivation/incentive packages, per diem rates, supervision protocols, and key messages) are reviewed and standardized across partners. ($1,000,000)

Improvement of case management in the private sector: Following up on a USAID-supported pharmaceutical sector mapping exercise, PMI will support a case management assessment of private sector providers and conduct targeted training to address key deficiencies identified in case management practices ($200,000).

Implementation of SMC: PMI will support the implementation of SMC in three districts of Kayes, continuing funding for a second year for Kita District (where SMC was financed initially with reprogrammed FY 2012 money) and including two additional districts. PMI will procure SP and amodiaquine for four rounds of treatment for children under five as well as cover additional implementation costs, including ASC training, supervision, and other support. Depending on the districts chosen, PMI will support implementation of SMC covering approximately 150,000 children under five. ($580,000)

Pharmaceutical Management

NMCP/PMI Objectives

Supply chain management: The People's Pharmacy of Mali (*Pharmacie Populaire du Mali [PPM]*) manages medicines for Mali's primary health care system and plans to cover more of Mali; reach more users; and reach international standards of warehousing, supply chain, and medicine provision. The PPM procures drugs through international tender from qualified suppliers and distributes them to the nine administrative regions. The PPM delivers commodities from the central level to the regional level but has no capacity to ensure reliable transportation of commodities to the community level.

The supply chain system is a combination of push and pull as the central level pushes down to the regions and the community health center staff pulls health commodities from the district pharmacies and CHWs obtain their health commodities from the community health centers. Although the districts are responsible for collecting commodities from the regional level, at times PMI has asked PPM to deliver directly to the districts for immediate supply at lower levels. The regions order monthly from the central level, whereas hospitals are on an automatic system of quarterly ordering. The district pharmacies purchase drugs from regional depots based upon monthly orders from health facilities (CSREFs and CSCOMs) and on the average number of drugs expected to be distributed within the district's catchment area.

If a drug is unavailable in the regional PPM stores, private pharmaceutical warehouses can fill orders. Ideally, the CSOMs keep one month of buffer stock and the regional drug depot (*dépôt répartiteur des cercles)* keep two months' worth. However, there are significant problems with drug storage at district depots related to storage capacity, humidity, security, and drug classification in warehouses. While CSCOMs must collect all required drugs from the district pharmaceutical depots, there is no central funding to support the transportation and logistics. The pull portion of the system still proves to be a great challenge, and commodities often do not reach the lowest levels of the health system. Multiple problems plague the Malian supply chain system and hamper the ability to maintain adequate supply. There is a lack of communication informing the district and community levels of the arrival of commodities at the central or regional level. At the CSCOM level there is limited funding to pay for transportation to pick up needed commodities, leading to stockouts, even when there is available stock in country. A key problem at the foundation of supply chain management is an overall lack of understanding of how to develop proper quantifications, order stock, and hold stock at the lower levels. Finally, the Bamako Initiative has created a governance issue that directly affects the provision of malaria commodities by creating disincentives. Pregnant women and children under five are supposed to receive ACTs for free under the Bamako Initiative; however adult medicines and other malaria medicines require payment to create a profit that is intended to support the supply chain system. Unfortunately, this has led to a disincentive for providers to order or offer free medicines as there is no financial gain. The negative incentive to request or prescribe free drugs has led to real and artificial stockouts. WHO and partners have begun discussions around the financial incentives issue to find a way to address the unintended consequences.

Regulation and drug quality: Several ministerial decrees provide guidelines for the management of pharmaceuticals in Mali. These include the formation of a national committee to oversee pharmacy retailers responsible for QC, inspection, and licensure and ensuring a basic package of pharmaceutical products. New standard operations procedures for pharmaceutical management were developed, but they need to be adhered to as there still appears to be minimal capacity, particularly at the lower levels of the health system. The National Essential Drug List is reviewed biannually. Laws are in place to ensure QC for imported drugs. The Directorate of Drugs and Pharmacies (*Direction de la Pharmacie et du Médicament* [DPM]) issues visas and imports licenses only after the exporter meets certification and other requirements. The National Health Laboratory (*Laboratoire National de la Santé*) samples drugs, verifies quality, and has regulatory authority to monitor pre- and post-market quality of drugs and other products, including insecticides and bed nets. Expired or poor quality medicines are destroyed at the national level. DPM, the National Health Laboratory, and customs meet quarterly to discuss regulations and importation or donation of medicines.

Pharmacovigilance: Pharmacovigilance is a high priority of the NMCP and the MOH. The Pharmacovigilance Department at the DPM has developed an action plan, adverse events notification form, and timetable. The plan has been implemented and trainings on adverse events notification and reporting have been conducted up to district level in all the regions except for Kidal Region. Adverse events reporting forms have been distributed to all public health facilities.

Progress during the last 12 months

Although the 2012 *coup* led to some disruption in malaria commodity availability, PMI Mali was still successful in getting commodities to the central and regional level, including sending emergency malaria commodities to the North through WHO. The political turmoil also caused some damage to the PPM warehouse in Tombouctou, which the PPM is currently in the process of rehabilitating. It will hopefully be ready soon so that the region can receive and store safely much needed commodities. During the past year PMI was the only major donor of malaria commodities as the Global Fund grant was still under suspension. This created gaps in supply, but PMI tried to assist through increased orders and emergency orders. In addition to updating, reviewing, and disseminating key documents such as the Essential Medicines Supply and Distribution Plan, a new standard operation procedures manual for the management of pharmaceuticals, An assessment of the logistics management information system (LMIS) began with FY 2012 funding, which will be used to provide recommendations for improvement of the system and developing standard operating procedures. Workshops and trainings were conducted to increase capacity in use of data for quantification and proper pharmaceutical and supply chain management. Advocacy for a national technical coordination committee continued and has likely reached approval; it should begin functioning within the next year. Monitoring stock closely and continuing to improve stock availability at all distribution levels still remain challenges. To support regular distribution of commodities, PMI supported the PPM to improve distribution of malaria commodities at all levels, including to the community level.

Challenges, Opportunities, and Threats

- Accurate quantification of malaria commodity needs is still a huge challenge in Mali as is effective distribution of commodities to the peripheral level. Distribution or request for commodities is often not seen as a priority by staff unless a financial incentive is included. The combination of a cost recovery system for adult medicines under the Bamako Initiative and the national policy of providing/delivering free antimalarials and treatment for pregnant woman and children under five create a rather complicated system of disincentives in which there is still inadequate funding to maintain a functioning pharmaceutical and supply chain system. Stockouts of malaria medicines at most levels outside the central medical store remains a great challenge, as does the distribution of commodities to the lowest levels of the health system.

- Improved communication and coordination among the PNILP, the PPM, the DPM, the district and CSCOM levels, and partners regarding supply chain issues, particularly quantification and distribution of malaria medicines, is needed to improve the flow of medicines and maintenance of stocks.

- With the return of the Global Fund as a key malaria commodity donor, PMI can focus again on filling gaps and assisting in ensuring a coordinated, full supply of malaria commodity needs.

Plans and Justification

PMI will continue to strengthen supply chain and logistics management including forecasting, quantification, and tracking of annual malaria commodity needs/gaps. PMI will work with the NMCP, MOH, and appropriate partners for improved coordination to ensure that essential life-saving drugs, including ACTs and RDTs, reach the end user. Support to the PPM in delivering malaria drugs and commodities to the regional depots will continue. PMI will establish a national coordinating committee to be led by the DPM with the participation of the NMCP, PPM, and supply chain partners, per recommendations from a supply chain workshop to improve the quantification and distribution of malaria commodities at the lower levels of the health system. PMI will also contribute to strengthening the LMIS system for better data availability and use.

Planned activities with FY 2014 funding ($500,000)

Logistics strengthening: PMI will continue to facilitate distribution of PMI-funded ACTs and provide technical assistance for pharmaceutical management, including forecasting commodity needs; distribution at central, district, and community levels; and improved coordination between the NMCP and PPM, through areas such as establishing a national medicines body comprised of all government organizations and partners involved in the supply chain system and providing medicines. Pharmaceutical and supply chain strengthening activities will include dissemination of guidelines, as well as national level training on the use of tools for quantification and monitoring of key antimalarial commodity availability at the facility and community levels. At the national level, use of the end use verification tool and the Procurement Planning and Monitoring Report of Malaria will be strengthened. This will entail continued training on pharmaceutical management and supply chain management standard operating procedures; quantification; ordering; and regular supervisory/monitoring visits of health facilities, CHWs, and regional and district warehouses. In addition, a feasibility study of private pharmacies and their role in malaria treatment will be conducted. ($400,000)

End-Use Verification Survey: PMI will conduct an end use verification survey to track essential commodities at the health facility level ($100,000)

BEHAVIOR CHANGE COMMUNICATIONS

NMCP/PMI Objectives

PMI supports harmonization of the national BCC strategy, ensuring consistency of messages and appropriate use of all communication channels and target audiences. While an updated national BCC strategy for the period of 2013-17 has not yet been developed, the current national strategy specifically mentions BCC messages targeted to vulnerable groups including pregnant women and children under five, as well as families and caretakers of children, CHWASCs, and the *relais*. The strategy also mentions key delivery channels for disseminating BCC messages such as radio, TV, mass media, and interpersonal communications. PMI-supported partners coordinate their BCC activities with the NMCP and the National Center for Information, Education, and Communication for Health and will work with these partners to develop an updated BCC strategy.

Progress during the last 12 months

PMI targeted BCC activities at community level through the *relais* (community health volunteers) and ASCs. These community cadres disseminate malaria prevention and control messages, conduct door-to-door health promotion visits, check the status of LLIN use, and target IPTp messages to pregnant women. According to the 2012 DHS, LLIN use is quite high (70% of children under five slept under an ITN the previous night and 75% of pregnant women slept under an ITN the previous night). PMI also supported the dissemination of a variety of pre-tested counseling materials and radio spots in local languages, as well as facilitated interpersonal communication through community groups. PMI partners developed subcontracts with different radio stations and teachers' training centers, and have trained more than 7,500 youth ambassadors against malaria. These youth ambassadors are school pupils trained and equipped to disseminate malaria prevention messages at school, within their families, and in the community. PMI partners also worked closely with women's groups, community leaders, and traditional healers to promote malaria prevention and control measures and encourage referral of sick patients to seek care at health facilities. During the annual World Malaria Day, PMI partners disseminated malaria BCC messages, including airing 14 television broadcasts on malaria prevention and distributing more than 2,500 brochures on malaria as well as linking malaria community mobilization activities with the African World Cup event in February 2013. PMI partners reported that the *relais* conducted 145,223 household visits to promote use of LLINs and referred 11,222 children under five to the nearest health facility or ASC for fever treatment.

Challenges, Opportunities, and Threats

- During the 2012-2013 political situation, PMI focused efforts on BCC activities conducted at the community and facility levels. Support for strengthening national BCC strategies has been on hold until USG policy restrictions are lifted. Aside from PMI, there is little direct support provided for malaria BCC activities since the Global Fund malaria grant has been suspended for the last two years. With the renewal of the Global Fund, PMI anticipates renewed support for BCC as well.

- PMI partners reported low community utilization and awareness of the ASCs' integrated health services package and responded by sensitizing and working with women's groups and strengthening the role of the *relais* to give BCC messages. Partners are also planning to organize health fairs at the district level to promote BCC activities.

Plans and Justification

PMI will support harmonization of messages and BCC activities at all levels to ensure consistency in technical messages and appropriate targeting of audiences. PMI will ensure that BCC activities for LLINs, MIP, and case management are implemented as an integrated approach under one program. PMI will work with other partners to explore ways to promote desired behavioral outcomes. PMI and partners will support alternative delivery channels for targeted BCC activities and messages including youths and schools, women's groups, community leaders, and traditional healers. PMI also intends to assist with updating and harmonizing the new national BCC strategy, working closely with the NMCP and the National Center for Information, Education, and Communication for Health.

Planned activities with FY 2014 funding ($420,000)

BCC for LLINs: Support for BCC activities will reinforce the correct use of bed nets throughout the year. While reported net usage is high during the high transmission season, efforts are needed to sustain usage during the low transmission season. Addressing the remaining barriers to correct hanging, use, and maintenance of nets and promoting year-round use is extremely important to help meet NMCP and PMI goals. Based on findings and recommendations from the recent study of the culture of net use study (described in the LLIN section), PMI will support targeted BCC messages to those who still do not use nets or are using nets seasonally, as well as encourage net repair and proper care and washing of a net. PMI will support partners to carry out multichannel strategies to communicate this information, including door-to-door messages disseminated by ASCs and *relais* in their communities. BCC coordination among PMI and implementing partners at the national and community levels is critical in order to ensure correct and consistent use of nets, uniformity of messages, regular monitoring, and subsequent reorientation as needed. PMI will support BCC activities following the LLIN distribution campaigns to increase the use of newly distributed nets by all age groups. In addition, PMI will support updating and harmonizing the new national BCC strategy, working closely with NCMP and the National Center for Information, Education, and Communication for

Health, to ensure BCC messages on net use are standardized across partners and monitor implementation of BCC messages. ($175,000)

BCC for MIP: PMI will support a multichannel strategy targeting pregnant women, women of child bearing age, and men, focusing on knowledge and perceptions related to MIP, women's awareness of risks of malaria during pregnancy, early and frequent ANC attendance at the CSCOMs, early use of IPTp in the second trimester, routine dosing with IPTp at every ANC visit, ensuring that LLINs are given free to pregnant women at their first ANC visit, and creating demand for proper treatment of MIP. These BCC activities will also include messaging for direct observation of SP administration for both health workers and pregnant women. PMI will continue to link BCC activities with HIV/AIDS messaging where appropriate. PMI will also support updating and harmonization of the new national BCC strategy, working closely with NMCP and the National Center for Information, Education, and Communication for Health , to reflect the new WHO IPTp policy recommendations. ($125,000)

BCC for case management: PMI will continue to support the dissemination of BCC messages related to case management through mass media and interpersonal communication and to harmonize malaria prevention and treatment messages. The strategy will promote early care-seeking for febrile children and compliance with treatment regimens. The ASCs and *relais* will also educate caregivers on signs of severe malaria that require prompt referral. PMI will support updating and harmonizing the new national BCC strategy, working closely with NMCP and the National Center for Information, Education, and Communication for Health to develop and implement communication approaches and messaging on malaria case management. ($120,000)

MONITORING AND EVALUATION

NMCP/PMI Objectives

Monitoring and evaluation is a key component of Mali's national malaria strategy, and the NMCP is focused on ensuring there is a coordinated plan for malaria data capture to inform programmatic interventions and measure outcomes and impact. A national malaria M&E plan covering the years 2007-2011 was developed, costed, and adopted in 2008, and an updated M&E plan for 2013-2017 has been developed. The current plan includes routine data collection and analysis through the national health information system, or SLIS; ESR; sentinel surveillance; and periodic national surveys to evaluate malaria prevention and treatment activities. PMI supports the NMCP's M&E strategy through its continued support for routine system strengthening, ESR, cross-sectional surveys, and internal M&E capacity building. While the general strategy itself has not changed, with the recent political events there is an increased emphasis on improving epidemic surveillance in the northern regions of the country and improving the quality and timeliness of routine data across the country.

The NMCP's Planning and Statistical Unit oversees all M&E activities, in close collaboration with health training and research institutions. Within the NMCP, the Division of Planning and Monitoring & Evaluation is tasked with developing operational plans and monitoring and evaluating program implementation. A second NMCP unit, the Division of Epidemiological Surveillance and Research, is in charge of promoting research on malaria, establishing an early warning system to detect and respond to malaria epidemics, and supporting operational units in epidemic response.

Routine System Strengthening: Mali's M&E system relies on malaria data collected routinely through the SLIS, but the quality of these data is variable and feedback is not delivered in a timely manner to assist program planning and management. SLIS data are compiled every three months and reported annually. These data theoretically include both confirmed and unconfirmed cases, but diagnostics are not routinely implemented. The 2012 data from integrated disease surveillance system, which does collect data on diagnostic confirmation, shows that on average 52% of malaria cases are confirmed in Mali, with the highest rate of confirmation in Segou Region (68%). The NMCP with support from the MOH has made a number of small-scale efforts to collect the number of confirmed malaria cases on a weekly basis; however, these efforts are not comprehensive and the data cannot currently be used to generate national-level indicators for malaria prevalence. In some cases the data are used at the local level for program monitoring efforts such as tracking the effectiveness of IRS campaigns. The NMCP hopes to increase the health system's capacity to collect, analyze, report, and use these data for programmatic decision-making. In the past few years, there has been a pilot effort, supported by PMI, to increase the timeliness and quality of the malaria component of the SLIS. In the most recent 6 months for which data are available, more than 95% of targeted facilities reported each month, and facilities using tally sheets decreased their compilation time from 15 hours to 4 hours per month. The plan for this pilot has always included an option to reincorporate this revised malaria system into the national SLIS, but the activity was stalled by political issues of the past year. In the upcoming year, the NMCP plans to expand this system to other districts and eventually to other disease areas as an enhancement to the SLIS system.

Household Surveys: Population-based surveys currently provide the most accurate data on malaria intervention coverage and malaria biomarkers (i.e., anemia and parasitemia). A national anemia and parasitemia survey conducted with PMI support in 2010 during the peak transmission period (Sept.-Oct.) provided the first parasitemia measures in Mali (see below for national estimates of anemia and parasitemia). A DHS including parasitemia biomarkers was conducted in 2012, and a health facility survey was also conducted in the high transmission season in 2012. This survey provides data on the quality of malaria case management and antenatal care.

Operations Research: PMI is supporting the roll-out of SMC at the request of the NMCP. In order to better inform the implementation of SMC under routine program conditions, PMI is conducting an evaluation of one pilot district over a 2-year period of implementation. The results will be used to guide decisions about the best approaches to implementing SMC in Mali.

Progress during the last 12 months

Despite the *coup* restrictions which prohibited direct financial assistance to the GOM for most of FY 2012, PMI and its implementing partners were able to show considerable progress during the year.

Routine System Strengthening: Prior to the *coup*, PMI, through its implementing partners, was supporting focused malaria routine system strengthening activities in ten districts in Bamako and Sikasso Regions. In collaboration with the NMCP, PMI supported revisions in data collection and reporting tools at 237 CSCOMs in focus districts. They also developed a malaria database and trained health workers and health officials in data collection and data entry at all levels. Two of the districts used SMS for data reporting from lower to higher levels, eight used paper-based reporting, but all districts entered the data into an online database, allowing for rapid analysis at the NMCP level. During the past year, PMI supported an assessment of the quality of the data in this system with very positive results. Greater than 95% of facilities report routinely each month into the system, showing 88% of suspected cases in children under five receiving a malaria diagnostic test. The system also tracks stockouts of key commodities. In March 2013 (the most recently available reporting period), 17% of facilities the targeted districts reported stockouts of ACTs, an improvement over the 25% of facilities reporting ACT stockouts six months earlier. At the same time, 34% of facilities were reporting stockouts of RDTs. The system has remained functional despite the suspension of technical assistance and has been a positive contribution to improved routine data in Mali. With FY 2013 funding, a study will be conducted to examine the comparative advantage of the SMS system vs. the paper-based tally sheets. The NMCP plans to expand this system to other regions of the country in the coming years.

Household Surveys: In 2012, Mali conducted a DHS survey which collected data on parasitemia and anemia prevalence, as well as intervention coverage indicators. Due to insecurity, the three provinces of the north were excluded from this survey. Preliminary data (final data have not been released) show that 84% of households own at least one ITN and 70% of children under age five slept under an ITN the previous night, roughly the same coverage levels as in seen in the 2010 A&P survey. Among women who had given birth in the last two years, 20% had received at least two doses of IPTp during their pregnancy. The proportion of children under age five with fever in the last two weeks who received ACT treatment within 24 hours was quite low at 2.5%[2]. While bed net coverage remained very high in Mali, the survey results for biomarkers of malaria and anemia were disappointingly high as well. Results reflect high transmission season estimates and showed that 52% of children 6-59 months of age were parasitemic by microscopy and 52% had severe anemia (hemoglobin 7-9.9g/dL). The high levels of both parasitemia and anemia, despite high intervention coverage, are concerning. PMI is currently investigating potential causes, such as higher than usual rainfall and the influx of displaced persons from the north, and hopes to have the results of this analysis available at the time of the release of the final DHS report.

Health Facility Survey: A PMI-supported health facility survey was conducted during the malaria transmission season in early 2013. The purpose of the survey was to measure the quality of malaria case management and ANC services in health centers by assessing availability and management of commodities, health worker knowledge of case management guidelines, and health worker practices related to diagnostics and prescriptions of ACTs and SP for pregnant women. The results provide important insights into case management practices in Mali. In particular, the survey highlighted incorrect diagnostic practices and insufficiencies in providers' knowledge regarding correct treatment, particularly for severe malaria. Approximately 37% of children under five with suspected of malaria were not tested by either RDT or microscopy.

Among adult patients, 55% were not told the correct number of days of treatment, and 41% were not told the correct dose to take. The results of the survey are being disseminated in country and used for improvement of training curricula.

The table below shows the main sources of data and sequence of surveys for malaria program monitoring and impact evaluations.

Data Sources for Monitoring and Evaluation in Mali, 2006 – 2016

Data Source	2006	2007	2008	2009	2010	2011	2012	2013	2014	2015	2016
Household Surveys	DHS				MICS A&P Survey		DHS (preliminary results available, final pending)			MIS	
Other surveys						RTI IRS Coverage Survey	EUV ATN Coverage survey	EUV ATN Health Facility Survey 2013	EUV	EUV	EUV
Surveillance and Routine Support	HMIS	HMIS	HMIS	HMIS	HMIS (incl: enhanced reporting from 10 districts)	HMIS (incl: enhanced reporting from 10 districts)	HMIS (incl: enhanced reporting from 10 districts)	HMIS (incl: enhanced reporting) ESR pending for North	HMIS (incl: enhanced reporting) ESR pending for North	HMIS (incl: enhanced reporting) ESR pending for North	HMIS (incl: enhanced reporting) ESR pending for North
OR/Other data sources					IRS Study on transmission delays Larviciding study	Barriers to IPTp Study Health financing for case management study	Culture of net use study				

DHS = Demographic and Health Survey; MICS = Multiple Indicator Cluster Survey; A&P = Anemia and parasitemia; MIS = Malaria Indicator Survey; EUV = End use verification; ATN = Assistance Technical National, bilateral nongovernmental organization; HMIS = health management information system

Challenges, Opportunities, and Threats

The greatest challenge for M&E activities in Mali is the political instability, including the insurrection in the north. If the elections proceed as planned in July and a democratically elected government is sworn in, many of the restrictions implemented following the *coup* will likely be lifted and PMI can resume normal relations with its GOM partners. However, several challenges will remain:

- It will take a new government time to appoint personnel to key positions, including positions within the MOH and NMCP. Once new staff are appointed, they will need to be oriented to activities and will likely have their own set of priorities for their agencies. The staff turnover and orientation of new staff will take time and focus away from rebuilding programs that were curtailed following the *coup*.

- The situation in the north of Mali remains unstable and USG activities are not authorized in the northern regions (Gao, Kidal, Tombouctou). While the northern region is sparsely populated and not malaria-endemic, this restriction still leaves three regions without support for potential malaria epidemics. This restriction may remain in place for a time even after a successful election process.

- The instability in the north has also caused a large number of residents to move out of the region, either to large population centers of southern Mali (Mopti, Segou, Bamako) or to refugee camps in neighboring countries. Because these individuals are from a non-endemic region, they do not have immunity to malaria that populations in southern Mali have acquired. Although the 2012 DHS did not collect information on IDP status, the data appear to support the anticipated increase in malaria burden as parasitemia among children under five has increased to 52%, from 38% in 2010. In addition, the region with the highest levels of parasitemia among children (71%) is the Mopti Region, where the majority of IDPs have settled. Therefore PMI anticipates an increased need for prevention measures (LLINs, IPTp) as well as increased cases in southern Mali for as long as the displaced persons remain there. PMI's reprogrammed FY 2013 funding as well as this FY 2014 MOP reflect these needs in the planning for commodities and activities.

Viewed through another lens, however, the readjustment of USG-funded activities to the community level actually presents an opportunity for PMI/Mali and other USG programs, to accelerate their reorientation towards improving health at the community level. Before the *coup*, there were pilot programs in various regions to support community case management integrated with other primary health services. During FY 2012 and FY 2013, PMI efforts focused on strengthening and expanding those efforts and will continue to support the integration of iCCM activities in the SLIS. After the political upheaval, USAID continued and strengthened its support for community-level health care provision. Monitoring and evaluation efforts have likewise focused on improving data collection at the community level and integrating the information into national systems.

Plans and Justification

After the political turmoil of 2012, and the hoped-for transition to a democratic government in 2013, FY 2014 will represent a new start for USAID/Mali. M&E activities will continue to play an integral role in responding to established PMI needs for program monitoring and impact assessment. With progress on SLIS in the pilot districts, there is a need to maintain the momentum by ensuring that health officers are equipped to use the data collected and that the database is user-friendly. This will ensure that data are disseminated and used to improve services. There is also a need to focus on data collection at the lower levels (CSCOM and even ASCs) to reflect the increased emphasis on programming at that level.

Planned activities with FY 2014 funding ($1,400,000)

Support for 2015 national household survey: PMI recommends that countries track coverage and impact through national-level population-based surveys every two years. Mali conducted a DHS in late 2012 to measure coverage of major interventions. This DHS also included parasitemia and anemia measurements to assess impact. Because these data only became available in 2013, the next household survey (likely to be an MIS) will be planned for 2015. ($500,000)

Routine system strengthening: PMI supports improvements in the M&E system at the CSCOM and CSREF levels in Mali to improve malaria data quality and use. In FY2013, PMI intends to build on accomplishments in improved routine reporting from health facilities by expanding the revised system to new areas. After expanding to Mopti in 2013, in FY 2014 the activity will focus principally on Sikasso, the most populated area of the country outside of Bamako. Activities in Sikasso will build on the results of strengthening activities in other districts focused on facility-based data collection. The efforts will also focus on continuing to build capacity at the local level to collect quality data and use the information for program improvements. The data collection system will be designed to incorporate data from iCCM sites into the regular SLIS reporting. For the most part, the expansion of the system will focus on the paper-based tally sheets which have been very effective. One of the activities will involve expanding the mobile data transfer system to key districts to facilitate timely malaria surveillance. ($450,000)

SMC implementation evaluation: In FY 2013, PMI began to support the scale-up of SMC in selected districts. Because there is little available data on the programmatic challenges of implementing SMC as part of a national malaria control program, PMI launched an evaluation of the SMC efforts it is funding in Kita District in FY 2013. The evaluation is intended to run for two years and collect data through two rainy seasons to control for seasonal variations in rainfall and transmission patterns, as well as through the inevitable challenges of implementing a new project. The funding in this line item is intended to support the second year of data collection for the evaluation of SMC. Funding for the drugs and implementation of SMC is covered under the case management section of the MOP and is not included here. ($150,000)

Therapeutic efficacy surveillance (TES): PMI recommends conducting therapeutic efficacy studies of first- and second-line ACTs every two years. In Mali, the Global Fund is supporting

TES activities but details of the plans, including sites and timing, are not available as yet. PMI intends to support a minimum of three sites to carry out therapeutic efficacy studies on ACTs for uncomplicated malaria. These sites will be developed as a complement to the Global Fund-sponsored sites. ($150,000)

End-use verification survey: PMI recommends conducting an end-use verification survey every year to track the availability of key commodities at the health facility level. This activity is funded in the case management section of the MOP.

EPIDEMIC SURVEILLANCE AND RESPONSE

NMCP/PMI Objectives

An estimated 1.5 million people in the northern areas of Mali are considered at-risk for malaria epidemics. This includes the 13 districts of the Tombouctou, Gao, and Kidal Regions and the northernmost districts of Mopti, Segou, Koulikoro, and Kayes Regions. The intensification of conflict in the north has created a migration of IDPs as well as refugees to neighboring countries. This movement of non-immune residents from the northern epidemic-prone regions to larger cities and towns in the central and southern endemic regions increases their vulnerability to malaria.

Past NMCP strategic plans included implementation of an ESR system for the north of Mali. Objectives were to detect 80% of epidemic episodes within two weeks of their appearance, and to control 80% of episodes within two weeks of their detection. The NMCP has created a new epidemic management plan for 2012 to address the current IDP crisis as well as the continued epidemic threat in the north. This plan identifies the target areas based on migration of non-immune populations, areas not yet covered by the rolling universal coverage campaign and experiencing increased rainfall, and traditionally epidemic-prone areas (i.e., the north). The plan includes strengthening routine epidemic surveillance by supporting all CSCOMs and CSREFs to systematically collect and report weekly malaria data; providing preventive measures (LLINs, IRS, SP) to areas at risk; organizing village health days; increasing BCC; ensuring case management through provision of ACTs, RDTs, and supervision; investigating all indications of malaria outbreaks; and ensuring a coordinated response by the district, regional, and national levels. It is important to note that the planned ESR is separate from the integrated disease surveillance system, which is a nationwide reporting system for notifiable infectious diseases and does not focus on detecting epidemics in specific regions or populations. Data from the integrated disease surveillance system are used at the national level and not for district-level response.

The periodicity of epidemics generally ranges from two to seven years with the most recent epidemic having occurred in 2013 in Tombouctou. During this time of conflict, the north has experienced interruption of health care services due to lack of health workers and destruction of health facilities. Areas that were normally at risk for epidemics due to ecological factors were at even greater risk of a health crisis because of the crippled health infrastructure; however, partners have continued malaria support in the north during the insecurity (for example, UNICEF sent ITNs, WHO and MSF supplied commodities, and other nongovernmental organizations supported malaria case management). The security situation is beginning to improve and PPM has rehabilitated the regional drug warehouse in Tombouctou.

Current data sources for malaria cases are inadequate for rapid detection of epidemic threats. Malaria data collected through SLIS are compiled only every three months and are thus not timely enough for epidemic surveillance. As mentioned above, the IDSR is a potential weekly data source for malaria cases, but health workers and district health officers are not trained to monitor and analyze the data to initiate an appropriate response as needed. There is also currently no consensus on epidemic thresholds for the northern regions.

Progress during the last 12 months

The NMCP has developed training guides for malaria epidemic management. The existing IDSR system currently reports suspected and confirmed malaria cases on a weekly basis, but the NMCP has little confidence that these data are analyzed at the district level. To date, there has been little progress on strengthening malaria ESR.

In response to the political conflict and migration of IDPs, PMI is using FY 2012 funds to strengthen ESR. These efforts began in the Mopti Region, where the largest number of IDPs from the north are concentrated and where PMI could still work under the *coup*, and will build on existing progress made in strengthening routine malaria data collection in Bamako and Segou. A PMI-funded consultant traveled to Mopti in June 2013 to establish a pilot ESR at three health facilities, including setting epidemic thresholds based on historical malaria data. The next step will be to expand the ESR system to the traditionally epidemic-prone northern region per the NMCP strategy for epidemic management.

Challenges, Opportunities, and Threats

Establishing a functional surveillance system is itself a challenging task, but Mali's northern regions impose additional challenges and threats:

- Ongoing security concerns limit the ability of implementing partners to move freely in this region to provide technical assistance for intervention activities.

- Health infrastructure in the north has been weakened due to health workers leaving the conflict zones, loss of supplies and drugs, and physical destruction of health facilities.

- Even in the absence of conflict, the populations, and thus health facilities, are spread across vast areas posing a challenge for supervision and data transmission.

There are also opportunities to facilitate establishing a functional ESR:

The collaboration will be led by WHO, which has extensive experience in establishing malaria surveillance systems. UNFPA and the European Union can also serve as key partners as they have supported the HMIS extensively.

- Pending future developments in Mali geared towards peace in the north, PMI and partners might be able to work directly in the north if the security situation improves.

Plans and Justification

With FY 2013 funding, PMI is collaborating with WHO and the NMCP to establish a functional ESR system in the north. This activity will build on the ESR system being piloted in the Mopti Region. The expansion of the ESR system from Mopti to the north will be a coordinated effort reflecting the NMCP's epidemic management strategy and incorporating lessons learned as appropriate. Specific ESR strengthening measures will focus on establishing epidemic thresholds, assessing existing data collection and reporting processes, revising these as needed, training health staff to analyze and monitor malaria data, and ensuring actionable response plans are in place. PMI will coordinate with the NMCP and other donors to ensure needed commodities are positioned for epidemic response.

With FY 2014 funding, PMI will support continued development of the ESR system, with a particular focus on ensuring capacity of local and regional health staff to report and analyze data in a timely manner.

Planned activities with FY 2014 funding ($150,000)

Strengthening epidemic surveillance and response: Through training and supportive supervision, build capacity of local and regional health system staff to collect, analyze, and report weekly surveillance data in a timely manner for epidemic detection and responding to epidemics in Mopti and the Northern Regions ($150,000)

HEALTH SYSTEM STRENGTHENING / CAPACITY BUILDING

NMCP/PMI Objectives

In 2007, the NMCP was elevated to directorate level, and it is now responsible for overseeing all malaria control activities conducted in Mali. The NMCP has four technical divisions which are Prevention and Case Management, Monitoring and Evaluation, Epidemic Surveillance and Operational Research, and Communication and Social Mobilization, as well as one administrative and financial division. The malaria focal point persons at regional and district levels are responsible for ensuring adherence to the national malaria guidance and implementation of the strategic plans. The NMCP organizes semester-long malaria review workshops with all the regions' focal points to monitor the implementation of the malaria activities, the adherence to national malaria policies, and the review of regions' malaria data. PMI contributed substantially to building capacity of the NMCP and other GOM entities through direct funding of specific activities and technical assistance from implementing partners.

Progress during the last 12 months

In FY 2012, due to the post*coup* restriction, all mission assistance to the GOM was suspended including PMI planned activities to provide capacity building to the NMCP and to strengthen the Malian health system. Most of the Mission's health projects and PMI activities were reauthorized to take place after months of suspension, mainly at community level. In this context, PMI was able to conduct training on FANC and malaria case management in the regions of Kayes, Sikasso, Koulikoro and Mopti. PMI supported the production and distribution of revised malaria and supervision guidelines and revised drug distribution guidelines in all regions, except for the three northern regions where security was an issue. Also, with authorization from the USAID Africa Bureau, PMI supported the DHS, which contained a malaria module to inform stakeholders on the country's health status. PMI also facilitated forecasting and quantification for malaria commodities and supported the training of four MOH managers in logistic management information systems.

Challenges, Opportunities, and Threats

- The recent political crisis in Mali triggered a USG suspension policy, which prohibited PMI from directly funding the GOM. If democratic elections are held by July 2013 and the USG restrictions on aid to the GOM are lifted, the USAID Mission will re-establish mechanisms to provide direct funding to the GOM.

- The MOH reports a critical human resources shortage at all levels of the public health system, especially for service provision below the national level. In addition, health workers are not distributed proportionately throughout the country. The shortage of staff, both in terms of quantity and level of training, affects the quality of service at each of these levels.

- Challenges for the NMCP include ensuring effective coordination among malaria partners, beginning at the central level, and training new staff in malaria control. In addition, the NMCP occupies a small, deteriorated structure with inadequate space for its 50 employees and poor electricity and internet facilities.

- Entomological capacity is fairly strong both within the MOH and at research institutes such as the University of Bamako's Medical School and MRTC. In 2009, the NMCP recruited a full-time entomologist, and has been engaged in the planning, analysis, and reporting of all activities supported by PMI, including IRS, entomological monitoring, and operations research. MRTC, supported by the U.S. National Institutes of Health, has over 50 malaria experts including laboratory scientists, epidemiologists, and entomologists. It has ongoing collaborations with the National Institutes of Health, University of California (at Los Angeles and Davis), Johns Hopkins University, Tulane University, Gates Foundation, and the WHO Africa Regional Office.

Plans and Justification

With anticipation that the suspension will be lifted after elections planned for July 2013, PMI will focus on building technical and managerial capacity at all levels of the health care system, both through implementing partners and direct support to the NMCP and other government partners through the government-to-government mechanism. Most inputs in training, supervision, and operational support are described elsewhere in the MOP.

Planned activities with FY 2014 funding ($50,000 plus additional costs referenced in other sections)

Strengthening NMCP functions: To help the NMCP reach its coverage targets for key malaria interventions, PMI will continue collaboration with other partners to support NMCP structure and staff, specifically to increase capacity at all levels to plan, implement, supervise, and forecast commodity needs; improve distribution systems; coordinate with partners; and monitor and evaluate malaria prevention and control activities. Strengthening NMCP managerial capacity will be critical as PMI supports scale-up of all interventions. In-country and headquarters PMI staff and implementing partners will continue to provide on-the-job training and support to improve NMCP management and coordination capacity. (A total of $195,000 referenced in other sections)

Direct support to NMCP for operations: Assist NMCP's day-to-day operations and ability to work closely with PMI and implementing partners. Will include support for a continuously functioning database and server for tracking malaria indicators. ($50,000)

Direct support to the NMCP and other government entities: Support will continue in assisting the NMCP and other government partners in FY 2014 to conduct training and supportive supervision in all malaria program interventions supported by PMI. In FY 2014, PMI will continue training and mentoring NMCP staff to increase their skills in data analysis, interpretation, and reporting of findings both from routine supervision and other data sources such as household and health facility surveys. Scopes of work for implementing partners will include provision, whenever feasible, for collaborating with the NMCP in building staff managerial and technical capacity. PMI will support the MOH Division of Public Hygiene and Health to conduct IRS-specific supervision and related environmental monitoring. In FY 2014 PMI will continue to support INRSP to conduct district-level refresher training, supervision in diagnostics, and perform QA/QC for malaria diagnostic in the 61 district health centers and the 1,134 community health centers. MRTC will be provided with funding to conduct therapeutic efficacy surveillance studies in three sites and conduct an evaluation of the SMC approach. (A total of $790,000 referenced in other sections)

The table below illustrates the proposed activities through direct support to the NMCP and other government entities:

Malian Government entity	Proposed activity
National Malaria Control Program	-Strengthen LLIN logistics and supervise LLIN distribution -Support NMCP entomologist in monitoring IRS operations and related entomological monitoring activities, -Support training and supervision visits to health workers at all levels and refresher trainings as needed -Support the day-to-day operations of the NMCP including the functioning of the malaria indicator database and server.
Division of Public Hygiene and Health	-Strengthen the capacity of DHPS to coordinate with the NMCP on district-level IRS operations and entomological monitoring.
Directorate of Reproductive Health /Midwives Association	-Engage the Reproductive Health Unit and midwives to increase awareness about MIP and free SP and strengthen and respond to barriers elucidated by recent assessment on MIP.
Malaria Research and Training Center	-Conduct therapeutic efficacy surveillance studies and evaluation of the SMC.
National Institute of Public Health Research	-Implement the QA/QC plan for RDTs and microscopy, including supervisions, and provide technical assistance to the refinement of the QA/QC plan and best practices for implementation.

STAFFING AND ADMINISTRATION

Planned activities with FY 2014 funding ($1,775,000)

Two health professionals serve as resident advisors to oversee PMI in Mali, one representing CDC and one representing USAID. In addition, one foreign service national works as part of the PMI team. All PMI staff members are part of a single interagency team led by the USAID Mission Director or his designee in country. The PMI team shares responsibility for development and implementation of PMI strategies and work plans, coordination with national authorities, managing collaborating agencies and supervising day-today activities. Candidates for resident advisor positions (whether initial hires or replacements) will be evaluated and/or interviewed jointly by USAID and CDC, and both agencies will be involved in hiring decisions, with the final decision made by the individual agency.

The PMI professional staff work together to oversee all technical and administrative aspects of PMI, including finalizing details of the project design, implementing malaria prevention and treatment activities, monitoring and evaluation of outcomes and impact, reporting of results, and providing guidance to PMI partners.

The PMI lead in country is the USAID Mission director. The two PMI resident advisors, one from USAID and one from CDC, report to the senior USAID health officer for day-to-day leadership, and work together as a part of a single interagency team. The technical expertise housed in Atlanta and Washington guides PMI programmatic efforts and thus overall technical guidance for both resident advisors falls to the PMI staff in Atlanta and Washington. Since CDC resident advisors are CDC employees (CDC USDD—38), responsibility for completing official performance reviews lies with the CDC country director who is expected to rely upon input from PMI staff across the two agencies that work closely day in and day out with the CDC resident advisor and thus best positioned to comment on the resident advisor's performance.

The two PMI resident advisors are based within the USAID health office and are expected to spend approximately half their time sitting with and providing technical assistance to the national malaria control programs and partners.

Locally-hired staff to support PMI activities either in ministries or in USAID will be approved by the USAID Mission director. Because of the need to adhere to specific country policies and USAID accounting regulations, any transfer of PMI funds directly to ministries or host governments will need to be approved by the USAID Mission director and controller, in addition to the PMI coordinator.

Table 2
President's Malaria Initiative - Mali
Planned Obligations for FY 2014

Proposed Activity	Mechanism	Budget		Geographical area	Description
		Total $	Commodity $		
PREVENTIVE ACTIVITIES					
Insecticide Treated Nets					
LLIN procurement	TBD	7,000,000	7,000,000	Nationwide (routine), Mass campaign (Segou)	Procurement of 2,000,000 LLINs: 1,400,000 for the 2015 campaign for Segou Region to complement other donors' contributions and contribute to LLIN delivery through routine services targeting children under five and pregnant women, and 600,000 LLINs for routine services.
Distribution of LLINs	TBD	1,500,000	1,500,000	Nationwide specific regions	Distribution and follow-up of LLINs for mass campaign (in Segou Region) and routine services to children <1 and pregnant women. Includes LLIN supply management, tracking, and forecasting for routine LLIN services.
LLIN logistics strengthening	NMCP	25,000	0	Nationwide	Support for coordination of LLIN supply chain management, tracking, and forecasting for routine LLIN services and for harmonization of LLIN IEC/BCC messages and activities.
SUBTOTAL ITNs		8,525,000	8,500,000		
Indoor Residual Spraying					
Indoor residual spraying	TBD (IRS follow-on)	5,100,000	1,500,000	3 Districts	Procure IRS equipment (insecticide, sprayers, etc.), training, implementation, data collection, protocols, guidelines, BCC, logistic assessment, technical assistance for spraying/entomological assessment (CDC IAA). Technical assistance from CDC entomologist for monitoring IRS implementation.
	CDC IAA	24,000	0		
Entomological monitoring	TBD (IRS follow-on)	300,000	0	3 Districts, Nationwide	Conduct annual entomological monitoring. Support the NMCP entomologist in conducting IRS-related entomological monitoring. Strengthen capacity of DHPS to participate in the monitoring of IRS operations, training of spray operators and to provide coordination with NMCP on district IRS operations. Mapping insecticide resistance and mosquito biting behavior nationwide.
	NMCP	20,000	0		
	DHPS (through NMCP)	40,000	0		

Activity	Description	Location			Partner
SUBTOTAL IRS			1,500,000	5,484,000	
Malaria in Pregnancy					
SP procurement	Procurement of SP to contribute to annual needs for all pregnant women.	Nationwide	270,000	270,000	TBD
Strengthen FANC and MIP services at the facility level	Roll-out new WHO IPTp recommendations and respond to barriers elicited during the recent assessment on IPTp barriers. Coordinate on FANC and MIP activities with the Reproductive Health Program and Midwives Association in the process. The latter will help with formative supervision, training, guideline development, and dissemination of guidelines.	Nationwide (and specific region)	0	425,000	TBD
			0	100,000	DSR/Midwives Assoc. (through NMCP)
SUBTOTAL MIP			270,000	795,000	
SUBTOTAL PREVENTIVE			10,270,000	14,804,000	
Case Management					
Diagnosis					
Procurement of RDTs	Procure approximately 1.5 million RDTs.	Nationwide	1,000,000	1,000,000	TBD
Quality assurance/quality control for diagnostics	Support implementation of QA/QC plan for RDT and microscopy diagnostics, including supervision. Provide technical assistance on refinement of QA/QC plan and best practices for implementation.	Nationwide	0	150,000	INRSP (through NMCP)
			0	12,000	CDC IAA
Formative supervision of laboratory technicians and clinicians	Provide refresher training supervision on microscopy and RDTs at the district level and selected lower level health facilities.	Nationwide	0	200,000	INRSP (through NMCP)
SUBTOTAL Diagnosis			1,000,000	1,362,000	
Treatment & Pharmaceutical Management					
Procurement of malaria drugs for uncomplicated malaria	Procure 1.2 million treatments of AL for health facilities, community case management and pregnant women.	Nationwide	1,724,000	1,724,000	TBD

Activity	Implementer	Amount 1	Amount 2	Location	Description
Treatment for severe malaria (injectable artesunate)	TBD	735,000	735,000	Nationwide	Procure 300,000 treatment packs of injectable artesunate (based on request from NMCP and HMIS estimate of 600,000 cases per year).
Training and supervision for case management	TBD	300,000	0	Nationwide	Training includes diagnostics, case management for simple and severe malaria, and supervision on all aspects of case management. A special focus will be placed on updating the guidelines, training, and supervision for severe malaria using injectable artesunate.
Training and supervision for case management	NMCP	150,000	0	Nationwide	Training includes diagnostics, case management for simple and severe malaria, and supervision on all aspects of case management. A special focus will be placed on updating the guidelines, training, and supervision for severe malaria using injectable artesunate.
Implementation of iCCM	TBD	1,000,000	0	All districts in Sikasso, Kayes, Koulikoro Regions	Implement integrated community case management activities in 3 regions
Improvement of case management in private sector	TBD	200,000	0	Nationwide	Following a mapping exercise of the private sector, support a case management assessment of private sector providers and conduct targeted training to address key deficiencies identified in case management practices.
Implementation of SMC (drugs and implementation)	TBD	80,000	80,000	3 districts in Kayes Region	Purchase medication for 4 rounds of SMC for 150,000 children under five in 2 districts of Kayes. Medication for 3rd district (Kita) already purchased with FY 2012 funds.
Implementation of SMC (drugs and implementation)	TBD	500,000	0	3 districts in Kayes Region	Implement SMC in three districts of Kayes.
Logistics strengthening	SIAPS	400,000	0	Nationwide	Strengthen pharmaceutical management and supply chain system at the national, district and community levels
End-use verification study	SIAPS	100,000	0	Nationwide	Tracking of malaria commodities down to the community level, end-use verification study with an emphasis on follow-up of findings.

Activity	Implementer			Location	Description
SUBTOTAL - Treatment & Pharmaceutical Management		5,189,000	2,539,000		
SUBTOTAL CASE MANAGEMENT		6,551,000	3,539,000		
Behavior Change Communication					
BCC for LLINs	TBD	175,000	0	Nationwide	Support BCC strategy harmonization and message design, including development of new national BCC plan.
BCC for MIP interventions	TBD	125,000	0	Nationwide	Support efforts to harmonize strategies and design focused messages to promote SP IPTp uptake and MIP targeting pregnant women.
BCC for case management	TBD	120,000	0	Nationwide	Continued support of messages and communications approaches for case management; implement through *relais*, train on referral systems at the community level with a focus on early care seeking behaviors. Support the National Center for Information, Education, and Communication for Health (CNIECS) capacity to develop and implement communications approaches and messaging for case management.
SUBTOTAL BCC		420,000	0		
Monitoring and Evaluation					
Support 2015 national household survey	TBD	500,000	0	Nationwide	Support Malaria Indicator Survey or Multiple Indicator Cluster Survey (or other national household survey) implementation and expenses in 2015; survey will include biomarkers.
Routine system strengthening (all levels)	MEASURE	450,000	0	Nationwide	Continue and expand routine system strengthening efforts with an emphasis at the CSCOM level. Evaluate data quality of SLIS. Support training and quality control/timeliness for completion of routine SLIS reporting forms, assist in analysis and feedback on malaria indicators and promote use of findings at all levels to improve program performance.
SMC implementation evaluation	MRTC	150,000	0	1 intervention district (Kita) and 1 control	Fund the second year of the evaluation of SMC implementation in Kita District compared to a non-SMC comparison district in Kayes. Evaluation will include household surveys for anemia and parasitemia and passive surveillance using facility data.

Activity	Partner	Location		Amount	Description
Therapeutic efficacy surveillance	MRTC	Nationwide	0	150,000	At a minimum of three therapeutic efficacy sites (complementing Global Fund TES funding), carry out therapeutic efficacy studies on first- and second-line ACTs for uncomplicated malaria
Strengthening of ESR	WHO	Nationwide	0	150,000	Strengthen capacity for conducting ESR in epidemic-prone districts
SUBTOTAL - M & E			**0**	**1,400,000**	
Capacity building					
Support day-to-day operations of NMCP	NMCP	National level	0	50,000	Assist NMCP's day-to-day operations and ability to work closely with PMI and implementing partners. Includes support for continuously functioning database and server for malaria indicators and communication means.
SUBTOTAL Capacity Bldg			**0**	**50,000**	
In-country Staffing and Administration					
In-country staff; Program Administration Expenses	USAID	Nationwide	0	1,400,000	Support for USAID PMI staff (1 PSC/1 FSN) with salaries, benefits, contribution to salaries and benefits of Mission support staff, IT support costs, office space, vehicles, other Mission program support costs, local costs for CDC PMI Advisor.
In-country staff; Admin. Expenses	CDC IAA	Nationwide	0	375,000	Support for CDC PMI Resident Advisor (1) with salaries, benefits.
SUBTOTAL - In-Country Staffing			**0**	**1,775,000**	
GRAND TOTAL			**25,000,000**	**13,785,000**